GREAT DAYS OUT

in Manchester and the Pennines

Janet Smith

Published by Sigma Leisure - an imprint of
Sigma Press, 1 South Oak Lane, Wilmslow, Cheshire SK9 6AR, England.

British Library Cataloguing in Publication Data
A CIP record for this book is available from the British Library.

ISBN: 1-85058-443-X

Typesetting and Design by: Sigma Press, Wilmslow, Cheshire.

Cover design: Martin Mills

Cartoons: Mick Davis

Printed by: Manchester Free Press

Disclaimer: the information in this book is given in good faith and is believed to be correct at the time of publication. No responsibility is accepted by either the author or publisher for errors or omissions.

Contents

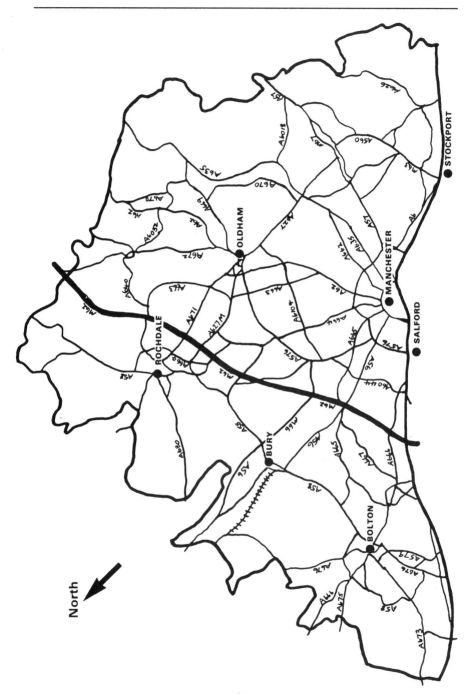

North

Welcome To
GREAT DAYS OUT!

This guidebook contains more than 100 attractions in the city of Manchester, Greater Manchester and parts of the Pennines. It includes the towns of Oldham, Rochdale, Chorley, Bolton, Stockport and Bury, and the area known as Tameside. And, unlike other guidebooks, it looks closely at the sort of facilities mums and dads need to know about when they are taking babies, toddlers and older children on days out.

As a parent myself, I discovered how difficult it is to take out small children – when you need to breast feed or find a cafe with a highchair or change a nappy.

And, as your children get older, their needs change – is there plenty to do, is it safe, could you spend a few hours or a whole day there?

I found other guidebooks lacking in what I thought was essential information – so I wrote my own.

This is the second edition of this particular guide – there are three in the series – and it has been updated, revised, added to, so that it is even better than the one before.

I've found several new places which I've checked out and included as well as updating the entries for the old favourites, always keeping in mind the needs of children from babies to school age.

I also looked at facilities for disabled people – mums with a disabled child must have twice or three times the problems that I do and need even more information before embarking on a day out. And lots of families want to take grandparents, some of whom might be in wheelchairs or have difficulty walking.

Although this guidebook is ideal for the visitor to the area, it is also intended for people who live there. Lots of the places listed are free and there are indoor and outdoor attractions. There is often a greater need to get out of the house when the weather is poor.

I have done my best to give full and accurate information, but, because facilities alter, opening times change and improvements are made, (or sometimes things are removed), I cannot be held responsible for alterations. So before you go, please check (I've listed telephone numbers) and make sure the venue is open at the times I state and the facilities you hope for will be provided.

When revising this book, I discovered that more places are providing nappy changing facilities, highchairs and other essentials – and it is this attention to detail that makes a day out with children into a Great Day Out. It has to be said, though, that some people I spoke to were not keen to provide nappy changing facilities because parents leave dirty nappies in the most unfortunate places. So please, if there isn't a bin provided, invest in a pack of nappy sacks and take it home with you.

If we as mums and dads don't make our needs known and continue to accept poor facilities when we are spending money at these places, things will never change. So let's make our voices heard – and maybe we can change the world a little for families with young children.

Hints For Travelling

TRAVEL SICKNESS

You may find that your Great Days Out are completely ruined by your child's travel sickness. It is a very common complaint in children and although nobody is absolutely sure what causes it, there are various theories. Some people say it is likely to affect a more excitable child, or one who is upset by the motion of swings and roundabouts so it could be associated with the mechanism of the inner ear which controls balance.

There may be signs when your child is as young as six months old or it may not begin until the age of two. It usually improves with age and by puberty may well be forgotten. But that's a long time to wait!

There are many ways to tackle the problem before then and we offer a few suggestions here.

▢ See your doctor. Discuss it with him or her. S/he may prescribe a drug to help, but these can have unpleasant side effects like a very dry mouth or overwhelming sleepiness.

▢ Try homoeopathic treatment. It is safe, inexpensive and can be used by anyone for minor health problems. Try your local health food shop or chemist The most popular remedy is *Cocculus* so try this first in either a 6 or 30 potency. The pills dissolve on the tongue and children readily take them. One or two doses should be given before the journey and then during the journey if symptoms return. Homoeopathic remedies should be placed on the tongue and allowed to dissolve. Do not take with food or wash down with a drink and allow 20 minutes before or after anything else is put in the mouth. (These remedies are not poisonous so even if a child swallows a whole bottleful, she will come to no harm.) If Cocculus does not work, you could try Tabacum or Petroleum.

▢ You can try to desensitize the child by going on short trips and gradually building up to longer trips. You may still need to give a remedy to help this.

▢ Don't let your child read or look at a book during the journey; this can bring on travel sickness.

▢ The child may be better sitting in the front if this is convenient, but only if big enough to be safely strapped in. Note: it is both unsafe and illegal to travel with a child on your lap – see Car Safety.

▢ Do not let YOUR child have large and/or greasy meals before a journey – but don't travel on an empty stomach either.

▢ Glucose sweets, plain biscuits and iced water are best for in-car snacks.

▢ Make sure there is a flow of fresh air during the journey.

▢ Allow for frequent stops.

▢ Make sure the child is properly fastened in so that she does not roll when the car goes round bends.

▢ Try games and activities during the journey that do not involve reading or moving about but that keep the mind occupied and off unpleasant symptoms. (see Keeping them Happy)

◻ Some mothers have found excellent results with the *Sea-Band*. Two bands are used on each wrist and it is said to operate by exerting a carefully controlled pressure on the acupressure point on both wrists. It takes from two to five minutes to become effective and continues to protect the wearer while being worn, claim the manufacturers. The Sea-Band is harmless and can be used by adults and children. It is said to provide effective nausea control for sufferers from all forms of motion sickness without side effects. It has been successfully used in pregnancies and in hospitals for post-operative nausea. Available at chemists or from Sea-Band UK Ltd., Church Walk, Hinckley, Leicestershire, LE10 1DW; telephone 0455 251007.

CAR SAFETY

More than sixty children are killed and more than seven thousand injured each year while travelling unrestrained in the rear of cars. The Department of Transport says that three-quarters of these lives could be saved and two-thirds of the injuries avoided if they all wore restraints.

If seat belts are fitted in the rear of the car, it is the driver's legal responsibility to see that they are used . . . not the mother's or father's, but the person who is driving the car, even if it is the first time you ever gave a child a lift.

The essential point is that the seat belt or restraint should be appropriate for the age and weight of the child. If it is not used by the child the driver risks a fine. (The child risks injury or even death.)

This is in addition to laws for drivers and passengers in the front seat, who must be restrained, whatever their age.

The Department of Transport says that ideally a child should be restrained in a purpose-designed restraint appropriate to the child's weight. The restraint will be labelled to show the weight for which it has been designed. The term "appropriate restraint" includes the following:

◻ For children under one year old, a carry-cot which is restrained by straps or an infant carrier (like the rear facing kind.)

◻ For children of one, two or three years old, an appropriate child seat or harness with booster cushion should be used with an adult belt.

◻ For children of four to 14, an adult belt.

It is also a good idea to establish good rules of behaviour in a car from the very beginning. And stick to them:

◻ If children unfasten their seat-belts, stop the car and refuse to go on until the seat-belt is fastened. Don't give in for an easy time. It could be critical to your child's safety. Once you begin saying: "It's okay just this once", you will find it harder to insist on the proper rules.

◻ If your car hasn't got child-proof locks on the back doors, have them fitted. And discourage children from fiddling with locks, handles and windows when you are driving.

◻ Never nurse a child on your knee in the front or back of the car while travelling. It is both illegal and unsafe, even if you are wearing a seat belt. And if the belt goes round both of you, the child will be crushed by your weight in case of a collision.

◻ The child must always be strapped in – even if screaming!

We have all driven with toddlers screaming in the back but try to put it into perspective: A 10-minute screaming fit while you drive home or to the nearest place you can stop safely is better than injury or loss of life if an accident happens.

KEEPING THEM HAPPY

Every parent knows how difficult it can be to travel even relatively short distances with children – especially if they are excited.

There are lots of things an older child can do in a car or on a bus or train, but with babies and under-fives it is more difficult.If you are planning one of our Great Days Out, try to organise your timetable so that those who still do have a day-time sleep are either sleeping on the way or on the way back. This is an enormous help if you can think ahead.

Of course, many parents also have the problem of NOT letting the child fall asleep on the journey – especially if you are returning home at 5pm and bedtime is 7pm. You arrive home weary and your little darling is bright-eyed and raring to go after an hour's nap! Try to keep her awake by playing music, talking or playing games if you can – although we know this is VERY difficult!

Either be prepared to accept this as the price to pay for a day out or alter your timetable. If it fits in with your day, you may like to travel home very late, so that sleeping children can be put straight to bed. In which case, consider taking their pyjamas, dressing gowns and night-time nappies and changing them before you leave.

Don't forget your emergency bag of:

❑   Loo paper and/or kitchen towel

❑   Moist wipes for faces, hands and bottoms

❑   Nappy changing equipment

❑   Juice in cartons with straws, feeder cups or whatever.

❑   Snacks such as apples, bananas, plain or salty biscuits, sultanas, raisins – definitely NO chocolate (it is so messy).

❑   Plastic bags just in case anyone wants to be sick (But keep plastic bags out of reach of all children).

❑   Potty – especially if in the middle of potty training or your child cannot manage adult toilets. Pack it in a plastic carrier bag with a snap-on clothes peg to hold it shut; wipe clean with a baby-bottom wipe if water is unavailable.

❑   Spare plastic bags for in-car waste, packing wet or dirty and discarded clothes etc. (They can even be used to sit on if the grass is damp for your picnic!)

❑   A change of clothing, right down to underwear.

❑   If you plan to return really late and there is a place for washing and changing before you leave for home, pyjamas and dressing gowns, so they can be popped straight into bed.

Games to play while travelling

For babies:

❑ Try sticking a picture to the back of the seat which the baby faces. We used to have an assortment of large, colourful or black and white pictures. They (surprisingly) keep babies fascinated for a long time.

❑ Try making cheap rattles with washed-out plastic bottles filled with rice or pasta. Glue AND tape the top for safety. Or fill with water and cooking oil for interesting effects.

❑ If someone is sitting next to the baby, play a peek-a-boo game with a tea-towel or coat.

❑ Use cardboard tubes and a ping-pong ball to play a "Where's it gone?" game.

❑ If baby can grasp, have a few old postcards or birthday cards to pass to the child.

For older children:

❑ Cut shapes out of card and pop them in a large envelope or paper bag. The child has to guess the shape without looking.

❑ All forms of I-Spy can be played. Look for red cars and blue cars and count them if the child is old enough.

❑ Take a kitchen timer and play "One minute's silence".

❑ Play a form of snap say with churches. When anyone sees a church they shout SNAP! (or a pub, or a type or colour of car etc.)

❑ Turn motorway travel into fun by shouting "Duck!" as you go under every bridge.

❑ Give children a clipboard with plenty of paper and crayons or pencils for drawing and colouring.

❑ Dot-to-dot books can be good fun for the child who is not prone to car sickness.

❑ Cut a postcard into a puzzle and have the child assemble it.

You can take a tray for these kinds of games, or some car seats have trays which fit onto them, to be bought at extra cost.

◻ Wrap small parcels of cheap surprise presents and at certain stages in the journey, give them to your toddler to unwrap. Expensive and time-consuming before you start, but well worth it on a long journey. Buy the cheap toys from market stalls etc, but make sure they are safe for your child's age group.

◻ Turn a hairbrush into a microphone and have the children give a running commentary on what they can see.

◻ Car bingo: if you have enough children, divide into two teams and given them each a list of things to spot. If they cannot read simple words, cut out, or draw pictures. List 10 items (a church with a spire, a church with a tower, a bicycle, a motorbike, etc) and make the 10th item a silly one, like an elephant. That makes the game even more fun – you'd be surprised how many toddlers can spot an elephant on a British motorway if it means winning the game.

◻ Use the car window: draw in the mist if it is that sort of day; or draw on the window with felt tips (it wipes off); or buy some cheap stickers that peel on and off.

◻ Music: buy cassettes of children's songs from places like the Early Learning Centre. They have saved the day for us on many a long journey. (Parents can't stand Humpty Dumpty for the tenth time but children can!)

◻ Get the children to make their own cassettes before you set off. Or make one for them with rhymes and jingles that you enjoy as a family. Or in a quiet moment, tape a story that they know well.

Admission Charges

Please note that charges quoted are valid for 1994. Prices may change, so do check. Remember that you can save money with family tickets and many more places are offering these now.

STD Codes

In April 1995, dialling codes will change to include a '1' after the initial '0'. The old and new codes are being used in parallel by BT. So – for example – you can use '0161' in place of '061' with immediate effect. The new codes are used throughout this book.

Disabled People

Most places welcome disabled visitors, but sometimes access is tricky and special arrangements have to be made – especially to stately homes and the like. Weekdays are always a better choice when there are fewer visitors. Companions of disabled or visually-handicapped people are usually admitted free of charge and the National Trust provides powered vehicles at many properties where access is steep or difficult.

Except for guide dogs, trainee guide dogs and hearing dogs for the deaf, you can expect that dogs are not admitted to many properties, parks and gardens:

For visitors to National Trust properties, a handbook for disabled visitors (including availability of Braille and taped guides, and the Sympathetic Hearing Scheme) can be obtained by sending an SAE to: The National Trust, 36 Queen Anne's Gate, London SW1H 9AS.

Tourist Information Centres

BOLTON: Town Hall, Victoria Square, Bolton. 01204-364333

BURY: Derby Hall, Market Street, Bury. 0161-705-5111

CHORLEY: Union Street, Chorley. 01257-241693

MACCLESFIELD: Town Hall, Market Place, Macclesfield. 01625-421995

MANCHESTER: Town Hall Extension, Lloyd Street, Manchester. 0161-234-3157

OLDHAM: Oldham Library, Union Street, Oldham. 0161-627-1024

ROCHDALE: The Clock Tower, Town Hall, Rochdale. 01706-356592

STOCKPORT: 9, Prince's Street, Stockport. 0161-474-3320

TAMESIDE; 32, Market Street, Ashton-under-Lyne. 0161-343-4343

MANCHESTER

THE MUSEUM OF SCIENCE AND INDUSTRY IN MANCHESTER

Liverpool Road, Castlefield, Manchester M3 4FP. Tel: 0161 832 1830

By car, follow the Castlefield signs in Manchester City Centre. The entrance is on Lower Byrom Street off Liverpool Road. Nearest station is Deansgate and the number 33 bus stops nearby.

Open 10am-5pm every day including Sundays and Bank Holidays except 23,24,25 December.

Admission £3.50 adults, £1.50 children (5-18), students, unemployed (UB40),over 60s and disabled; children under five free. (Prices until March 1995).

Car parking on site is £1.50 per car.

This is a very busy and enjoyable place – don't let the word "museum" put you off! We took two four-year-olds and a two-year-old and they thoroughly enjoyed it. But for older children, it is a must. Make this a full day out to get your money's worth.

There are 15 galleries to explore but perhaps the most exciting for young children is Xperiment! which is on the top floor of the Lower Byrom Street Warehouse. This is a hands-on science centre – children can explore light and energy by looking, pushing and pulling levers, pressing buttons and even walking inside a large camera. There is a corner specially for the under fives here – but our testers enjoyed the whole lot.

The Air and Space Gallery is also fun for small children; there is a Super X Simulator (additional charge) in which you can experience the sensations of flight – but under fives are not allowed. However this is more of a warning because some children may be frightened.

You can experience "Underground Manchester" and walk through a Victorian sewer, see steam mill-engines at work, look at nuclear power and electricity, printing, machine tools ...

In fact, you do need a full day to explore everywhere.

Lots of staff available to help and advise.

It is accessible for pushchairs and wheelchairs virtually everywhere with lifts or ramps – and they are welcome.

The Museum Coffee Shop (first floor,Lower Byrom Street Warehouse) has highchairs and will heat bottles and baby food if asked. Packed lunches may be eaten in certain areas.

Toilets in the Air and Space Gallery and at several places in the Lower Byrom Street Warehouse. Toilets for the disabled available on ground, first and second floors. Nappy-changing room (with lock) is by the ground floor entrance to the Lower Byrom Street Warehouse and can be used by mums or dads and can be used for breast-feeding.

MANCHESTER AIRPORT
(See *Further Afield* for The Aviation Viewing Park)

Ringway, Manchester. Tel: 0161-489-3000; for special tours: 0161-499-0303

M62 west-bound leave at junction1/12 for the M63; leave M63 at junction 9 for M56. Follow signs to Manchester airport.

Open daily.

Parking – short stay and long stay. Free coach parking for tour groups.

Free admission to airport. See below for special tours.

An interesting day out for children who enjoy aircraft or a worthwhile trip before you embark on a foreign holiday by air. Park in the short stay areas and look for signs to the spectators' terrace. Lots of steep steps to climb. Often very breezy here. We found that toddlers see the aircraft better from mum's or dad's shoulders so expect to do lots of lifting and carrying with small ones. Shop selling aircraft memorabilia. Basic toilets nearby.

Inside the airport, viewing is possible from main lounge area. There are several places to eat and drink, all expensive. Highchairs available.

Toilets inside including for disabled people. Very good mother-and-baby room with lots of easy chairs for feeding, highchairs if you want to spoon feed, nappy changing facilities, plenty of paper etc.

For schools, guides, brownies and adult groups, there is a tour centre with tour guides. Inside the centre there are constantly changing displays by the major airlines, plus many items depicting facets of aviation, past and present. Tour groups can see aviation videos on a wide screen system. Each tour lasts about two hours and is tailored to suit your group. Costs about £25 minimum for a group although it is possible for groups to be made up of individuals when the charges are adults £2.50, children £1.50. Contact the tour telephone number if you are interested. Special meals can be laid on for tour groups.

CHILDREN'S WORLD

Central Retail Park, Great Ancoats Street, Manchester. Tel: 0161-274-3818

Open weekdays 10am-8pm; Saturdays 9am-6pm; also Sundays and Bank Holidays 11am-5pm.

Free parking.

Free admision.

Children's World belongs to the Boots Group and offers almost everything for the under fives under one roof – toys, games, books,clothes, baby requisites, prams, pushchairs, playpens etc.

Parking is easy, access on the flat. You can take your pram or pushchair round the store and into the toilets and mother-and-baby room. This is an excellent way to shop if you have to take young children with you. There is a large safe fun slide, a soft play area and other entertainments at special times (i.e. Father Christmas). The snack bar has good wholesome and fun food for children, cartons of juice, feeder cups, serves jars of baby food, lots of highchairs and will warm babies bottles. The mother-and-baby rooms have excellent feeding and nappy-changing facilities and the toilets feature small toilets for young children as well as low-level wash basins and hand dryers.

CASTLEFIELD GALLERY

Liverpool Road, Castlefield, Manchester . Tel: 0161-832-8034)

By car: close to Mancunian Way or follow signs to Castlefield in city centre. Bottom of Deansgate.

By bus: Castlefield is served by bus routes from Piccadilly Station, Piccadilly Gardens, Arndale Centre and Albert Square. Bus no. 33 stops on Liverpool Road.

By rail: Deansgate Station.

Open Tuesday – Friday 10.30am-5pm, Saturday noon-5pm, Sunday noon-4.30pm.

Free admission.

Car parks nearby (Watson Street and Water Street.)

This is a very small gallery of contemporary art which stages Saturday morning workshops for 6-12 year-olds run by artists. It's a fun, hands-on workshop, practically-based. £2 for first child, £1 for other children in same group. Telephone to check – but workshops are held most Saturdays throughout the year.

Small ground floor accessible for pushchairs and wheelchairs. Steep stairs to lower ground floor – inaccessible. Toilets.

GRANADA STUDIOS TOUR

Water Street, Manchester M60 9EA. Tel: 0161 833 0880

Well signposted from all over Manchester City Centre: follow the brown and/or yellow signs.

Open all year. Closed Mondays in summer and Monday and Tuesday in winter. Open Tuesday to Sunday 10am-4pm April 1 – Sept. 30. Wednesday to Sunday 10am-3pm Oct 1 – March 31.

March 29-June 30 and Oct 1 to March 1995 prices are: Adults £10.99 children 5-11yrs £7.99. July 1- Sept 30 prices are: Adults £11.99, children £8.99. Under fives free. OAP discounts in Jan, Feb and March.

Parking opposite entrance and in Water Street, £3 per car.

Great fun, very slick and very enjoyable if a little pricy – but worth it for a treat. The backstage one-hour guided tour gives you a peep behind the scenes at the making of television and film – see Number 10 Downing Street, the giant's room, Coronation Street, Baker Street, Checkpoint Charlie. We took a two-year-old who was interested in bits here and there; a three-year-old in our tour was quite frightened at times and that might apply to anyone up to five. But older children will find this a super day out.

It is expensive, but you can spend all day there. After the tour there are lots of places to eat, from smart dining rooms to Diners. For young ones there's the Sooty Show and older children can enjoy MotionMaster, advanced technology cinema, 3-D cinema, scary live shows and even a seat in the House of Commons. A really full day.

Eating places vary – but we found children's portions in the restaurant. Highchairs, staff will warm bottles. No picnic site.

Toilets at various points; toilets for disabled people; good nappy-changing and breast feeding room near the entrance.

We took a pushchair on the tour and it is possible, but it does get in the way. Wheelchairs are welcome as are disabled children but Granada Studio Tours would like prior notice to ensure the best assistance. Ramps next to stairs. First aid officer.

15

CASTLEFIELD CARNIVAL

Castlefield, Manchester.

The Castlefield Carnival is held annually in mid-September and consists of two open days at the Castlefield attractions, street entertainment, crafts, children's play area, boat trips, stalls and sideshows. Contact Castlefield Visitor Centre (Tel: 0161-834-4026) for details.

BRIDGEWATER PACKET BOAT TRIPS

The Bridgewater Canal, off Liverpool Road, Castlefield, Manchester..
Tel: 0161-748-2680

Follow signs to Manchester Museum of Science and Industry: opposite the main entrance is the Castlefield Hotel which is situated by the canal basin. See bus and rail routes to Museum above.

Open Easter to Christmas for group bookings, Easter to clocks going back for public trips from Worsley village, Sundays only.

Parking on meters in Liverpool Road; car parks in Water Street opposite Granada Studios. Parking at Worsley village by the canal.

Group hire from £120 – £165 depending on length of trip. Public trips: adults £2, children and pensioners £1, under fours free.

The group trips go from the canal basin opposite the Museum of Science and Industry. Schools and other parties often include the boat trip in a day visit to the museum. Trips are either two and a half or three and a half hours and can be booked by telephone. The Bridgewater Packet is a smart, traditional narrow boat with seating and tables. There is a full commentary during the trip, toilets on board and a bar selling drinks, soft drinks, teas, coffees, snacks.

Public trips go from Worsley Village. Take the East Lancs Road A580 from Salford: left at Worsley Road; canal is near to the roundabout in the village. The trips last one hour in a more rural setting, travelling to Boothtown and back. Bar facilities and toilets. No nappy-changing facilities.

Pushchairs can be folded and stored on the boat. Some wheelchairs can be accommodated but it means removing seating, so telephone in advance.

16

IRWELL AND MERSEY PACKET COMPANY

Sails from landing stage opposite Granada Studio Tours (see above); office is at 84, Hayfield Road, Salford 6. M6 8QA. Tel: 0161-736-2108. Ship's 'phone: 0831-179519

Follow signs from Manchester to Granada Studio Tours: the boat sails from the landing stage at the rear of the car park.

Public trips operate most days except in poor weather. Also private charter.

Fares: adults £3, children under 12 and oaps £2, babes in arms free.

Parking at Granada Studios (see above.)

The centrally-heated Princess Katherine seats 80 passengers and sails from the landing stage up river and then to Salford Quays and back – about one hour. In summer there is forced air ventillation with a sliding roof. There are toilets on board, room to store pushchairs and snacks and drinks are available. No nappy-changing facilities. Disabled people can be carried onto the boat but Stan Salt who runs the boat prefers them to sit in seats rather than in a wheelchair on board. School parties by arrangement. One trip offers a cruise to Salford Quays Heritage Centre, plus lunch at Harry Ramsden's (see below). Contact 0161-832-9144 for details.

HEATON HALL AND PARK

Prestwich, Manchester, M25 2SW. Tel: 0161-773-1085/5388

Off the A665, north of Manchester at Prestwich or off A576, Middleton Road. Exit junction 18, M66.

Park open daily. Check Hall opening times on 0161-773-1231.

Free admission to hall and park.

Car parking free during the week but 50p per car weekends and Bank Holidays. Coaches £5.

The Hall and Park belong to Manchester City Council. In good weather you could spend a whole day here seeing the hall, enjoying the park's facilities and the farm. Hall has several period rooms, fine

17

plasterwork and paintings but opening times are restricted due to lack of staff. Please check before setting out. (0161-236-5244)

Toilets upstairs in the hall, but plenty in the park including for disabled people. Nappy-changing in large toilet block.

The park has acres of rolling land – plenty of room for ball games, picnics etc. Boating on the lake, children's playground, golf, pitch and putt, donkey rides, pony trekking, regular activities including a family fun day. The farm centre has live animals and machinery as well as an acivities room and special arrangements can be made for school visits. (Contact Jean Dowler 0161-773-1085). Children's farm parties also available to include pony rides. Also look out for the steam spectacular, fairground organ rally etc. Vendors selling food in the park and vending machines in farm centre. Staff will supply hot water for bottles and non-fizzy drinks are available.

Most areas are accessible with pushchairs and wheelchairs. Steps in the farm but only to the hatchery.

WYTHENSHAWE HALL AND PARK

Northenden, Manchester, M23 0AB Check for opening. Tel: 0161-236-5244

Off Princess Parkway, A5103, for junction 3 of M56 then exit 9, M63.

Opening times erratic due to lack of staff. Always telephone first.

Free admission.

Car parking free during week, 50p per car at weekends.

This is a half-timbered, furnished Elizabethan house and gives children an idea of how people used to live. Two of the areas have no ropes so you can get really close to exhibits. School visits can be arranged. Toilets including for the disabled.

The park is enjoyable although smaller than Heaton (above); tropical plant houses are fun with a fruiting banana tree to see. Children's playground and events throughout the season including a family fun day.

MANCHESTER CITY ART GALLERIES

Mosley Street and Princess Street, Manchester M2 3JL. Tel: 0161-236-5244

In the heart of Manchester on corner of Mosley Street and Princess Street, 200 metres from town hall.

Car parking in Lower Mosley Street.

Open daily 10am-5.45pm. Sunday 2pm-5.45pm

Admission free

This is a large, family-friendly art gallery that welcomes people to see its paintings, sculpture, ceramics, silver, glass and furniture as well as displays and exhibitions. Workshops for adults and children during the year as well as family events, mostly around Christmas time. Worksheets for older children. Schools welcome. For more information about special activities telephone extension 143 and for schools, ext. 146

Access is a problem in this 1815 building which is approached by steep flights of steps and which cannot accommodate a lift. Staff are keenly aware of this but their hands are tied. Ground floor and first floor linked by yet more stairs. Be prepared to carry disabled people and/or babies, pushchairs etc.

Cafe with highchairs but no special children's meals. Gallery shop. Toilets including for the disabled and nappy changing facilities on ground floor

SALFORD MUSEUM AND ART GALLERY

Peel Park, Salford, M5 4WU. Tel: 0161-736-2649

Signposted from M602 or follow signs for hospital and university in Salford. Situated on A6 approx one-and-a-half miles north of Manchester. Salford Crescent station quarter of a mile

Open Mon-Fri 10am-4.45pm, Sun 2pm-5pm

Car parking including disabled parking

Admission free

This is a large friendly building with plenty to do on a wet afternoon.

The main museum exhibit is a period street called Larkhill Place, typical of a northern industrial town at the turn of the century. This is a wonderful reconstruction with street scenes, shops and homes and makes a super learning experience for children of all ages.

The art gallery permanently displays a collection of works by L.S. Lowry which are very accessible even if art isn't really your "thing." Well stocked shop.

Events held for the family throughout the year, sometimes on a Sunday afternoon and are well worth attending. Events are free and materials provided. Ask for leaflets. Very smart and pleasant coffee shop serving everything from drinks to light meals. Highchairs, bottles warmed, children's portions and non-fizzy drinks

Pushchair and wheelchair access to all parts including use of lift. Toilets including Radar key for disabled; table in ladies' toilet for nappy changing. No breast-feeding facility.

MANCHESTER UNITED MUSEUM AND TOUR CENTRE

Sir Matt Busby Way, Old Trafford, Manchester, M16 0RA. Tel: 0161-877-4002

M63 Junction 7, follow signs to Manchester City Centre

Open Tuesday to Sunday 9.30am-4pm. On match days, 9.30am to kick-off

Car, coach and disabled parking. Admission: tours and museum – adult £4.95, juniors/oaps £2.95, family ticket £11.95

Museum only – adults £2.95, juniors, senior citizens £1.95, family ticket £6.95. Under fives free. Pre-booking required for ground tours.

The museum covers the history of United since its inception in 1878 in words, pictures, sound and vision, right up to the present day. If there is a football fanatic in your family, this is a great day out. There are more than 400 exhibits including trophies, kits, footballs and shirts. The tours are hourly and last approx one and a half hours, taking visitors to the press centre, stadium control room, players' lounge and dressing rooms. You may even sit in the manager's seat. Take a camera (although there is camera hire if you forget) as you may be able to have your photograph taken with a favourite player (without actually meeting him!) Be prepared to spend in the souvenir kiosk. For a party with a difference, enquire about birthday tours

Pushchair and wheelchair access to most areas. No facilities for babies, toilets including for disabled people. Disabled children welcome. Coffee shop but no highchairs or feeder cups.

HARRY RAMSDEN'S

1, Water Street, Manchester, M3 4JU. Tel: 0161-832-9144
Follow brown tourist signs to Castlefield and Granada Studio Tours
Car, coach parking and disabled parking
Open Mon-Sat 11.30am-11pm, Sun 11.30am-10pm

This is a 200-seater licensed restaurant with waitress service, plus take-away, and is founded on the famous original Harry Ramsden's at Guiseley, near Leeds. Haddock and chips, bread, butter, tea or coffee is £5.10, but there are other fish choices on the menu as well as a vegetarian dish of the day, steamed sponge puds, ice cream etc. Under 12s children's menu is £2.99 for haddock or sausage or fish bites and chips, with bread and butter, peas or beans and a soft drink followed by ice cream. Children under seven are given a Postman Pat menu with a word search, crossword and dot-to-dot to occupy them whilst waiting for food. (However in my opinion it is more suitable for five yrs and upwards, unless younger ones can simply colour it in.) Highchairs, feeder cups, bottles warmed – all very child friendly.

Wheelchair and pushchair access to most parts, no stairs and access from the car park is on the flat. Nappy changing and feeding facilities, toilets including for the disabled.

SALE WATER PARK CYCLE RIDE

For further details contact the Cycling Project for the North West, Environmental Institute, Bolton Road, Swinton, Manchester, M27 2UX. Tel: 0161-794-1926

Starting point is the Mersey Valley Visitor Centre (see below) just off M63 junction 8. Train travellers alight at Dane Road Station and the leaflet gives the short route from the station to the circular cycle ride. Also from Manchester or Bury on the Metrolink Tram – but no bikes allowed on the tram

Free parking in at least five adjacent car parks.

Free admission

This four-mile circular bike ride is to help the inexperienced or family group get on their bikes. A great day out if you can get the family's bikes into the boot of the car – or you may live near enough to cycle there. It's within easy reach of Sale, Stretford or Chorlton. Most of the route is over tracks which may be bumpy or muddy. There are also a few barriers over which you may have to lift your bike. They are there to prevent motorbikes gaining access. The Cycling Project advise you to pump up your tyres hard before you leave.

THE MERSEY VALLEY VISITOR CENTRE

Sale Water Park, Rifle Road, Sale, M33 2LX. Tel: 0161-905-1100

M63, junction 8. Turn left off Rifle Road. By train, alight at Dane Road. On Metrolink tram service from Bury or Manchester.

Open Tuesday to Sunday 10am-4pm. Closed Mondays and Christmas Day.

Car parking

The centre has a seasonally changing display and a varied programme of walks, talks and events. There is an information desk and a cafe which opens weekends and every day during the summer. The area is rich in wildlife and there are usually water sports taking place on the lake so there's lots to see. Most of the paths around the lake are accessible with wheelchairs and pushchairs. Friendly wardens are on site and it is a popular, often busy place to walk. There is a fine nature reserve with a hide for public use and the centre has a good relationship with local naturalists who report their sitings for the What's About board.

MERSEY VALLEY SHORT WALKS

Starting point: Mersey Valley Visitor Centre, see above.
How to get there – see above.
Free parking

There are several walks around this area with accompanying leaflets, from one to five miles in length. Most are self-guided with marked trails. The footpaths round Sale Lake are accessible for wheelchairs and pushchairs, but wheelchairs would have difficulty on the walks mentioned here. The paths are blocked by stiles to prevent motorcyclists using them. Strong people could lift pushchairs over. For further details call in at the centre.

THE SALFORD LOOP LINES – FOR CYCLING

For further information and a leaflet to show the exact routes, contact the Cycling Project for the Northwest, Environmental Institute, Bolton Road, Swinton, Manchester, M27 2UX. Tel: 0161-794-1926
M62, junction 13. Starting point is Monton Green, near the church.
Limited on-street parking around the Green. Nearest railway station is Patricroft.
Follow Green Lane into the village.
Free admission

The route follows the course of the old railway line with the lower arm called the Tyldesley Loopline to Ellenbrook and the upperarm the Roe Green Loopline to Little Hulton. It is a 5.5 mile loop with 1.75 mile extension round trip to Ellenbrook on the Wigan boundary. Or you can take the 2.5 mile return trip to Little Hulton on the Bolton boundary. Most of the routes are along converted disused railway lines. There is a section on residential roads and another on a shared pedestrian cycle lane. There are some barriers en route, but these are to prevent access for motorbikes. The route claims to be for inexperienced cyclists and family groups.

Before you set off, pump up your tyres hard and check your brakes.

The looplines have rapidly become a wildlife corridor, encouraging free movement of plants and animals into the heart of urban areas. A variety of trees and shrubs have been planted to enhance the area for wildlife. There are beech woodlands at Worsley Woods (no cycling), Parr Fold Park with recreational facilities (again no cycling) and you may like to stop and take a a look at Ellenbrook, with the church of St. Mary built in 1725.

OLDHAM

DELPH, UPPERMILL, DIGGLE AND DOBCROSS

For more information contact Saddleworth Tourist Information Centre, Saddleworth Museum, High Street, Uppermill. Tel: 01457 874093

Delph is on the A62 from Oldham; for Uppermill take A669 from Oldham and turn left onto A670. Dobcross and Diggle are both signposted from the area, but offer few attractions. Free car parking at both Delph and Uppermill.

These four places are in the Tame Valley area and come under Oldham Leisure Services. Delph and Uppermill are worth visiting but have become popular tourist areas and are very busy on Sundays.

Leaflets and information about the areas can be obtained from Saddleworth Tourist Information, including walks etc.

DELPH has a small car park in Millgate and otherwise, parking is difficult. The public toilets are at one end of the village with a Radar access toilet for disabled people. No nappy changing facilities.

There are several interesting little shops selling gifts and food, as well as small galleries and waterside walks. Getting round the village with a pushchair is difficult – narrow, uneven paths. But you can walk by the water and feed the ducks (which can sometimes be a little threatening and greedy.) Local interest trail available price 75p from Saddleworth Museum and some local shops. The Gallery Tea Room in King Street offers quality home cooking and is welcoming to families. It is small, but wheelchairs and pushchairs are welcome – one step to negotiate. Bathroom upstairs where it is possible to nappy change. (01457 874705). Crafts are sold at the front of the cafe. The riverside Shore Mill coffee shop (01457 873725) is in a Grade 2 listed building and serves cakes, sandwiches, etc; tables inside and out. Woodys Vegetarian Restaurant in King Street opens evenings only (01457 871197).

UPPERMILL is a larger village with shops, galleries, craft centres, as well as cafes, restaurants and pubs. Parking available at the museum, civic hall and baths but for relatively few cars. Be warned –

parking is a nightmare at busy times, usually Saturdays and Sundays. Uppermill's shops and attractions tend to close Mondays and Tuesdays. Narrow pavements make getting about with a pushchair difficult. There is a small park in the centre of village with baby swings, slide, roundabout with soft surfaces. The canal has a whole colony of ducks and geese, eager for food. There is a museum and art gallery (see below) and boat trips (see below). The Alexandra Mill Craft Centre has a fascinating array of small shops selling everything from books to children's clothes, art, furniture etc. There are two cafes – both have highchairs – and one offers children's portions on some meals. Toilets, but not for disabled people.

DIGGLE is not as pretty as the other villages, but is a good base for walks along the canal. Follow the signs for Diggle Ranges along Sam Road and you will come to Diggle Field. You can park here and walk the two miles to Uppermill along a canal towpath which although muddy at times is fine for wheels. The Diggle Hotel welcomes children and has a children's menu. On fine days youngsters can play in the small garden at the front of the pub. Access up two low steps, wheelchairs welcome, but no toilets for disabled people and no nappy changing facilities.

DOBCROSS is an extremely pretty village with numerous weavers' cottages, clothiers' and merchants' houses and a village square virtually unchanged in 200 years. Worth a look.

SADDLEWORTH MUSEUM AND ART GALLERY

High Street, Uppermill, near Oldham. Tel: 01457-874093

A669 from Oldham and M62 junction 20. Buses from Manchester, Oldham and Huddersfield. On main street (A670) through village; watch for signpost.

Open March-October Monday to Saturday 10am-5pm, Sunday noon-5pm. November-February, daily 1pm-4pm.

Free parking outside but limited numbers.

Admission adults £1, children and OAPs 50p. Family ticket £2.50. Under fives free.

The museum has several different sections including the gallery which introduces the visitor to the Saddleworth landscape and its

26

history. The Victorian rooms are particularly interesting and the machinery in the textile rooms can be seen working on certain Sundays in the summer. A fascinating display of bicycles, motor bikes and cars. It's a lively display which children will enjoy.

The museum has an education officer and school parties are welcome. Activities for children during the holidays. A visit here could be linked with a canal boat trip – see below. The art gallery has temporary exhibitions changing throughout the year.

Both museum and art gallery are reached by a steep flight of stairs – but a chair lift may be installed in 1994. Once up the stairs it is partly accessible to pushchairs and wheelchairs but there is an alternative interior route and staff will help where possible. Women's toilet on ground floor, suitable for disabled people, locked – ask at reception for key. Men's toilet on upper floor. No nappy changing facilities.

CLOUGH BOTTOM NURSERIES

Dobcross New Road, Dobcross, near Oldham, OL3 5NP. Between Delph and Uppermill at Dobcross. Tel: 01457-876571

Open daily.

Free car park. Free admission.

This is a nursery and garden centre in a beautiful country setting which actually welcomes children. It's not a high-tech presentation but pleasantly rural. There are usually animals to see – goats, pigs, rabbits, turkeys, hens etc. – which keep children amused. The nursery grows its own bedding plants and sells a range of shrubs, trees and garden accessories. A new building houses garden equipment and a coffee shop, selling home-made cakes, teas, ice creams etc with tables in and out. Difficult but not impossible for either wheelchairs or pushchairs although ground and pathways are uneven.

Footpath from car park takes you on a 10-15 minute walk to Uppermill (see above) and a footpath through a gate in the opposite direction takes you along the stream, across a bridge and, by forking left, to a playing field and children's small play area.

Basic men's and women's toilets. No nappy changing facilities or toilet for disabled people.

PENNINE MOONRAKER

Uppermill, near Oldham. Contact John Bradbury at 10, Hill End Road, Delph, near Oldham, OL3 5JA. Tel: 01457-873085.

Located on canal behind Saddleworth Museum and Art Gallery on High Street, Uppermill. Follow signs for museum.

Usually open April to October, Saturday, Sundays and Bank Holidays but don't expect the boat to be there on a poor day. Charter bookings in and out of season.

Parking in museum car park – limited spaces. Otherwise, very difficult.

Public trips – adults from £2.20, children from £1.10 return. Family saver £5.50.

Ask Mr Bradbury to quote for charter bookings.

Pennine Moonraker is a 70-foot long narrowboat which cruises along restored stretches of the Huddersfield Canal currently between Wade Lock/Uppermill Basin and Wool Road Basin, Dobcross. The return journey negotiates two restored locks and traverses three levels of waterway. The trip takes a slow one hour – very peaceful – and the boat allows a maximum of 50 passengers (minimum number for party bookings 25.) There is full cover from the weather which doesn't restrict views. Commentary for private bookings only, not on public trips. Central heating, flush toilet, refreshments. No special facilities for disabled people, but people in wheelchairs have been lifted on and off and have enjoyed the trip. Available for schools, parties etc. Ducks to feed – could be linked with a trip to Brownhill Visitor Centre (see below) or Saddleworth Museum (see above.).

BROWNHILL VISITOR CENTRE

Wool Road, Dobcross, Oldham. Tel: 01457-872598

On the Huddersfield - Uppermill Road, near junction with Delph New Road at Dobcross.

Open weekdays May to September 10am-4pm, October to April 11am-4pm. Closed Mondays except Bank Holidays. Saturdays and Sundays open May to September 10am-5pm, October to April 11am-5pm.

Free parking in front of centre or further along Wool Road.

Admission free.

This is a truly child-friendly place and although small, has lots to look at to fire the imagination. Tanks containing a variety of creatures which children can study and a crawly tunnel for both adults (a tight fit for some!) and children to see what life is like for animals underground. A creatures of the countryside display. Upstairs there are changing exhibitions and always something to do for children. Staff welcome arranged visits from playgroups and school. These can be linked with a visit to Saddleworth Museum and a trip on the Pennine Moonraker canal boat (see elsewhere in the Oldham section.)

Outside in a few small acres, there is the canal, a pond, dry stone walls, hedges, wetland, meadow land, beehives etc as well as a picnic area. Children – with an adult – can borrow nets and buckets and enjoy pond dipping.

There are summer and winter activities at weekends and during the week, many for families. Ask for leaflet.

No refreshments, although picnic area. Stairs to upper floor.

Toilets outside, including for disabled people. No nappy changing facilities.

TANDLE HILL COUNTRY PARK

Tandle Hill, Royton, Oldham.

For Countryside Ranger service, tel: 0161-627-2608.

M62, exit 21; A663 to centre of Royton and turn right at traffic lights along A671 to Tandle Hill. Signposted left. Entrance is along Tandle Hill Road which seems built up and unlikely to take you to the park – but it does.

Open daily

Car parking – limited. Two spaces for disabled people.

Admission free.

Tandle Hill Country park is a delightful wooded, hilly and scenic park, super for a Sunday afternoon walk or a full day out if you're armed with a picnic.

There is an attractive board at the car park giving details of the paths from which to choose. A perimeter walk is suggested for dog owners, and wardens are trying to improve the dog dirt problem by providing poop scoops in a box at the entrance. If you have a dog, please take one of the special bags with you at the start.

We took the shortest route with granny, pushchair and two small children and it took us a good two hours. However, if you have older children and stride out, you could get round in just over an hour.

But you can spend much longer by meandering through the wooded areas, bird spotting and stopping at the edge of the park to see the magnificent views. The war memorial can be reached by a new stepped route, or up a steepish pathway. A signpost gives you an idea of the landmarks that you can see in the distance.

Some paths are wide and covered in Tarmac, but almost everywhere is accessible with a pushchair if you are adventurous – and perhaps a wheelchair too. Although a special, short viewing run for wheelchair users has been created from the centre.

The new centre which replaces the old fire damaged one, has good toilet facilities, including for disabled people, but no nappy changing facilities. There could be a cafe here when you go – when we returned to check the area, the cafe was yet to be opened. The park also has a pitch and putt course.

DOVE STONE RESERVOIR

Signposted off the A635 Holmfirth to Mossley road near Uppermill.

Open all year round.

Free parking

Free admission

If you enjoy dramatic scenery, this is a spectacular place. You can walk all round the reservoir and the path is wide and well surfaced so it's possible for pushchairs and wheelchairs. The distance is three to four miles so it might take a couple of hours with small children. Stopping for a picnic is a good idea. There is a map and information at the car park, as well as toilets and a Radar toilet for disabled people. No nappy changing facilities and no refreshments.

THE OLDHAM WAY

This is a 42-mile circular walk, linking places of interest along the Oldham boundary. The route is indicated by distinctive owl symbols on signposts and can be walked in stages as all-day rambles or as afternoon strolls as it has been divided into seven different sections. Route guides describing each stage have been produced by Oldham Metropolitan Borough Council and are available at visitor information centres or the Tourist Information Centre at Oldham Library (0161-627-1024). We have spoken to a couple of people who have taken small children on stages of this walk, but it needs careful planning and you need to know your child's limitations.

OLDHAM ART GALLERY AND LIBRARY

Union Street, Oldham, OL1 1DN

For the museum, tel: 0161-678-4653; for library, tel: 0161-678-4643. (Tourist Information is now in the library on 0161-627-1024.)

In centre of town, five minutes walk from bus station and shopping areas.

Open Tuesday 10am-1pm, Wednesday to Saturday 10am-5pm, Sunday 1pm-5pm, closed Mondays.

Parking behind the building in pay-and-display car park.

Free admission.

Magnificent Victorian building houses both library and art gallery. Good children's library. Gallery has changing contemporary exhibitions and also works from its collection. School parties welcomed, workshops on Saturdays and Sundays but not always for children. Pushchairs and wheelchairs are welcome, but access is extremely difficult. The building is approached from the outside up a huge flight of stairs. Side entrance has lift access and any member of staff will help – but you have to send someone into the building first to ask.

There is an enclosed garden with floral borders, trees and benches.

Art Gallery Cafe serves light lunches as well as coffee and cakes. Highchair, will heat up baby food and bottles. Open every day except Tuesday (which doesn't coincide with the art gallery) 10am-4pm.

Public toilet at entrance. Toilet for disabled people in library. No nappy changing facilities.

OLDHAM MUSEUM

Greaves Street, Oldham, OL1 1DN. Tel: 0161-678-4657

M62 and A62 from north west to Oldham; A62 from Manchester and Huddersfield.

Open Tuesday 10am-1pm, Wednesday to Saturday 10am-5pm, Sundays 1pm-5pm.

Parking behind museum – 200 pay-and-display spaces. Five minutes walk from bus station.

Admission free.

The museum has changing exhibitions on human and natural history. In the basement, there is a charming recreation of an Edwardian street scene which uses the small space extremely well. There are noises and smells, voices of people talking in the pub, which all help to create a lively atmosphere. Well worth a visit for children. Shop selling souvenirs.

Access is difficult as there are stairs, but where possible the museum has installed ramps and a lift. Access to the basement is restricted however. The place is small enough for a toddler to walk round so you could forget your pushchair. People in wheelchairs would do well to telephone to see how they can be helped.

Cafe in the art gallery next door. See above for opening times.

Toilets in the art gallery next door – there is a way through so do ask. Toilets for disabled people in the library next door, or nearest in town's bus station. No nappy changing facilities.

The museum and art gallery have an enclosed garden with floral borders, trees and benches.

TOWN SQUARE SHOPPING CENTRE

Town Square, Oldham. Tel: 0161-678-6216
Signposted in town centre.
Open Monday to Saturday 9am-5.30pm.
Parking for 450 cars. Five minutes from bus station.

This is a shopping centre where the needs of parents with young children have been incorporated into the planning. Access from the car park is by lift. Spacious malls, usual town centre shops, ideal for pushchairs or wheelchairs.

Country Larder cafe has highchairs, will warm babies' bottles and has food for children.

Toilets at car park entrance FGH for able bodied. For disabled people and those who need to change nappies, locate the area between HMV record shop and H. Samuel's. It's quite high-tech and a little disconcerting for first timers, because you have to press a button to connect you with the control room. They can see you and check you are a legitimate disabled person or a mother and baby – and then they let you in. The NCT approved facilities have a sink, dryers, chair, nappy-changing table, emergency free nappies, breast feeding etc. Boots and Mothercare in the shopping mall also have changing and feeding rooms.

THE SPINDLES

Town Centre, Oldham.

This is another, newer shopping centre, which is fine for families and people with pushchairs and wheelchairs. Wide malls, usual town centre shops and lifts and escalators to take you up or down.

The food court on the first floor has a children's area with fun "train seating", lots of highchairs and a lift to that area. Staff will heat up bottles and jars, they sell baby food, children's burger boxes, jacket potatoes, etc. The only trouble is that you could not handle a pushchair and baby and tray complete with food. But staff say they will help mums and wheelchair users.

Toilets including for disabled people. Nappy changing facilities on first floor with shelves, sink, hand-dryer, nappy dispensing machine, and two feeding chairs behind a screen.

ALEXANDRA PARK

Park Road, Oldham (for information ring Tourist Information 0161-627-1024). A 15 minute walk from town centre or look for the A672 south of Oldham. Park Road is nearby.

Open all year.

Free car park.

Free admission.

This is a splendid park, built to give the unemployed something to do when the American Civil War threatened Oldham's cotton industry and therefore its lifeblood. It's worth getting a copy of the Alexandra Park Trail guide (from Tourist Information) if it is your first visit as it has intriguing and humorous notes on the park, its statues and history.

You must walk along the Top Promenade considered at one time to be one of the finest walks in the country – it is lined with more than 80 black poplars. There are two massive boulders in the park too – one originated in Ice Age Scandinavia and was carried to Oldham by glacier.

There is a paddling pool, boating lake open in season and another lake, home to hungry ducks and geese. The children's playground is disappointing. Bowling, tennis, conservatory, putting.

Lots of activities for children in the park, usually in school holidays. Check with Tourist Information (0161-627-1024) or Glodwick Pool (0161-633-7126.)

Toilets at Park Road entrance including for disabled people and near paddling pool.

GLODWICK POOL

Nugget Street, Oldham. Tel: 0161-663-7126

From Oldham town centre bear right to Glodwick Road; near to Mumps. Pool is set back behind the main road, so watch out for a smallish new building.

Car parking. Buses 414,425,426.

Open Monday to Friday mornings 9am-noon; Monday and Wednesday afternoons 1pm-7.30pm; Tuesday afternoon 1pm-6pm; Saturday 8.30am-12.30pm; Sunday 9am-11.30am. These times will vary during local school holidays.

Admission from 75p for children and £1.35 for adults.

This is a very friendly pool – small but beautiful! There are lots of activities throughout the week including aqua natal, mother and baby and children's activities during school holiday such as canoeing, football, netball etc. Ask for details.

Swimming tuition for most age groups after school.

Disabled access throughout with easy access to the pool as it is graded from nothing to 1.7 metres, gently sloping. Groups of disabled people use the pool regularly. Super for small children to gain confidence.

Baby changing tables, play-pen in female changing, pushchairs may be brought to the side of the pool.

Can be hired for children's parties on Saturday and Sunday afternoons – very popular.

DUNWOOD PARK

Small Brook Road, Shaw, Oldham. For Countryside Ranger service and more details, tel: 0161-627-2608.

A663 Milnrow Road, Shaw by Small Brook Road which leads to the car park. Nearest bus stop at the junction of Small Brook Road and the Milnrow Road, 200 yards from park entrance. Phone GMPTE 0161-228-7811 for information. Railway station at Shaw which is one mile away via Beal Lane, Milnrow Road and Small Brook Road.

Car park free.

Open daily

Free admission.

This is a park with pathways through woodland and hillsides with views across the Beal Valley. It adjoins an old formal park with a bowling green, tennis courts and a children's play area with soft surfaces. (However, there is a super new children's play area a short five minute walk away. Go across the railway bridge leading from the park and cross the main A663 – carefully- into another park. This has imaginative play equipment for all ages under 10 with soft surfaces.)

You can park off the road near the play area or drive a little further up Small Brook Road and park in the car park, where there is an information point and picnic area. This area includes an access route for pushchairs and wheelchairs in the lower valley area. There is a wild flower meadow, seating and picnic area. The woodland area is steep but you can follow an easier route along the valley floor next to the River Beal.

Lots of bird life, some beautiful trees, a lovely walk.

No toilet facilities.

DAISY NOOK COUNTRY PARK

John Howarth Visitor Centre, off Stannybrook Road, Failsworth, Oldham..
Tel: 0161-308-3909

A627 from Ashton-under-Lyne, turn down Newmarket Road, right again at
Stannybrook Road and immediately right into Boodle Car Park.

Open Tuesday to Friday 1pm-4pm. Saturday and Sunday 10.30am-5pm.

Free parking.

Free admission.

This is a good base for exploring the countryside of the Medlock
Valley near Oldham. There are ponds, the canal, footpaths, bridleways, woods, a lake, wildlife including rare water birds and lots of
easy walking. Get a free trail map before you set off.

Horses keep to bridleways which are often churned up and
muddy, but footpaths are clear and accessible in the most part with
wheelchair and pushchair. Sammy's Basin and the model boat pond
are ideal for sailing toy and model boats and Crime Lake has some
rare and fascinating water birds. The arboretum has seating for picnics and Boodle Wood, though difficult for wheels, has a pleasant
pathway through. You can take a circular walk or continue through
and under the A627 to Park Bridge Visitor Centre (see below) which
would take about one and a half hours. Lots of family activities in
winter and summer.

The cafe opens all week in the summer, weekends in winter, selling
ice cream, teas, burgers, snacks etc. Limited facilities but eager to help
people with special requirements.

Daisy Nook Centre has toilets, including one for disabled people,
but no nappy changing facilities.

THE MEDLOCK VALLEY WAY, a 12-mile way-marked walk
stretching from the centre of Manchester to the Oldham Moors, passes
by Daisy Nook centre (see above.) The route is tremendously varied
with river and canal-side stretches throughout reclaimed areas,
clough woodland and open country. The route can be walked as a full
day ramble or a series of shorter walks. A Walker's Guide (£1.50) is
available from Tourist Information and visitor centres and the local
Medlock Valley wardens will help with further details. There are
plenty of car parks and access with public transport. Contact the

warden service at The Stables, Park Bridge, Ashton-under-Lyne, OL6 8AQ. Tel: 0161-330-9613.

ROYTON ASSEMBLY HALL

Market Square, Royton, Oldham, OL2 5QD. Tel: 0161-620-3505.

Two miles from Oldham along A627, 1 mile from A627(M). Motorway link-up three miles to Rochdale along A627.

Open 10am-2.30pm weekdays. Saturday 10am-1pm. And various other days depending on functions.

Car parking.

Admission varies.

This is a multi-purpose hall with a wide variety of shows for all age groups. But there are many for children in the lively and entertaining programme. We've seen several shows here and have always been impressed. Leaflets available give age suitability for children and there are shows for the under fives. Contact the above number for details or ask to be put on the mailing list.

Pushchair and wheelchair access to ground level in main hall.

Kiosk selling tea, coffee, sweets, ices etc.

Toilet for the disabled. Main toilets down a flight of stairs. Nappy changing facilities and will arrange an area for breast feeding mums.

SADDLEWORTH CIRCULAR CYCLE ROUTE

For more details contact the Cycling Project for the North West, Environmental Institute, Bolton Road, Swinton, Manchester, M27 2UX. Tel: 0161-794-1926.

The Saddleworth circular offers three routes and hopes to encourage the inexperienced cyclist and families to get on their bikes.

The routes are graded, but all can start from either Greenfield Station or near the Royal George Public House, at a lay by situated next to the junction of the B6175 and the A635. Quiet roads, disused railway lines or tracks which may be bumpy and muddy are used. All three of the routes involve crossing or riding on an A road for short sections. If in doubt, dismount and push your bikes.

Route One is an easy 4.5 miles, Route Two is seven miles and moderate and Route Three is 10 miles and difficult. Contact the above address for the leaflet and detailed map.

You cycle near to Brownhill Visitor Centre which has refreshments and toilets and there is a tea shop at Diggle for route two.

GRANGE ARTS CENTRE

Rochdale Road, Oldham, OL9 6EA. Tel: 0161-624-8012
Situated in the grounds of Oldham College, Rochdale Road, Oldham.
Box Office open weekdays 10am-noon, 1pm-4pm. Closed Saturday and Sunday unless there is a performance.

The theatre is now run by the college and is the home for local amateur companies and college student productions. Amateur shows include musicals which are for family entertainment and there is usually a Christmas pantomime. There is a free mailing list or you can pick up leaflets around the town.

Coffee bar and bar open during performances only.

Access to the theatre for wheelchairs and special facilities for disabled people. Toilets, including for disabled people. No nappy changing facilities.

ROCHDALE

CHAMBER HOUSE URBAN FARM

Rochdale Road East, Heywood, Rochdale, OL10 1SD. Tel: 01706 48710

From Exit 20, M62 follow signs to A627(M) Rochdale, then A58 to Bury. Or left at Tesco roundabout, right at next roundabout to Heywood and Bury; Chamber House is red brick building on left opposite cemetery. Buses 470 or 471 from Rochdale bus station – stops outside farm.

Open daily April to Sept. weekends 11am-4.30pm, weekdays 1pm-4.30pm. October to March 1pm-4.30pm. every day.

Admission free, donations welcome.

Free car park.

Chamber House is a truly working farm with a herd of pedigree Jersey dairy cows and a flock of pedigree milk sheep. The 66 acres are managed as a commercial unit but it is owned by Metro-Rochdale and there for your enjoyment. Child friendly and welcomes playgroup visits. There are other animals to see including ducks, pigs and geese. Sheep are usually milked in season at 1.30pm and cows at 7.30 am and 3.30 pm. Visitors can watch. Short nature trail, best in spring, ideal on foot for very small toddlers.

Playgroups, school parties welcome. Question sheets available. Also, if your child has allergies or food intolerance, ask for their leaflet on the value of sheep milk products which can be bought in the shop, including sheep's milk ice cream which our two-and-four-year-old testers loved.

Rough, uneven paths but possible with wheelchairs and push-chairs, except access to upper viewing gallery.

Lots of "specials" – watch out in local Press – including carol service, sheep shearing, craft days, dry stone wall building etc.

Cafe serving snacks and drinks, with highchairs, feeder cups and non-fizzy drinks. Picnic site. Gift shop.

40

Toilets including disabled and nappy-changing facilities. Office made available for breast feeding if needed.

Springfield Park is across the road – see below.

ROCHDALE'S PARKS

ROCHDALE has three good parks which are well worth visiting with small children. They are not necessarily "days out" but are a useful way of passing an afternoon with a toddler or a little longer if you take a picnic. Springfield Park is very near Chamber House Farm (above) so you could combine the two for a day out. It is possible to walk from Springfield Park to Queens Park – it would take about three quarters of an hour with a young family.

SPRINGFIELD PARK

Marland Road, Rochdale.
Take Marland Road from Tesco roundabout in Rochdale.(See farm directions above.)
Open daily.
Free car parking.
Free admission.

This is a large, enjoyable park with plenty of open space, a running track and golf course. There is a fenced pond with ducks to feed and a delightful model railway run by enthusiasts, which is to be extended this season. It opens Easter to October on Sundays. Excellent children's play area with imaginative equipment and sand for soft surfaces. A walk of about one-and-a-half miles by the River Roch through woodlands and open countryside joins Springfield Park to Queens Park (see below).

Toilets, no nappy-changing but some access for disabled.

QUEENS PARK

Queens Park Road, Heywood.
Open daily.
Free car parking.
Free admission.

This park is ideal for youngsters with a good children's play area with fun equipment, swings and soft surfaces. There is also a pet's corner with ducks, geese, rabbits, chickens and an aviary with budgies. Band concerts in the summer.

Toilet facilities; cafe open seasonally.

FALINGE PARK

Shaw Clough, Rochdale. Take A58 from Rochdale, turn left at A680 Spotland Road and right at Sherriff Street B6377.

Open daily.

Free car parking. Free admission.

This is a well kept park which is being improved all the time. The children's play area is particularly good and includes a cone-shaped "spider's web" for climbing. The current equipment includes soft surfaces and is excellent for the under-fives and older children. There is a small conservatory with interesting plants and a display area outside. There is usually a special event on weekends during the summer – band concerts, garden parties etc. Car boot sales once a month on Sundays. The Friends of Falinge run the cafe on event days selling snacks like scones and sandwiches. This is also available for birthday party hire. No highchairs. Toilets including disabled people in the cafe.

Other toilets are housed in a temporary building; key available at the conservatory 12-4pm Saturday and Sunday only. No facilities for the disabled.

(For more information about Rochdale's parks, telephone 01706 350459 during office hours.)

LITTLEBOROUGH COACH HOUSE AND HERITAGE CENTRE

Lodge Street, Littleborough, Lancs OL15 8BA. Tel: 01706-368481

Follow signposts to Heritage Centre from Littleborough's main through road.

Open Saturday 11am-4.30pm; Sunday 2pm-4.30pm; Tuesday-Friday 2pm-4.30pm. Monday closed.

Free admission. Free car parking.

The coach house is a Grade 11 listed building and dates from the 18th century. It was originally built to serve the busy horse-drawn coach traffic on the main transport routes into Yorkshire over Blackstone Edge and also through Todmorden. It is staffed by volunteers and fund raising keeps it open. There are books, displays, sometimes art exhibitions and things to buy. Activities such as aerobics and dancing are held here.

To be honest, there's not much to see and very little to entertain small children. But there are family events throughout the year such as Christmas festivities and the traditional "Pace Egg" Easter play staged here. Look out for details in the Rochdale Observer.

Rooms to hire for parties.

The cafe is well worth a visit with good home cooking in a spacious dining room. Children are welcome, one highchair, small portions of food given gladly and will heat up bottles and baby food. Sunday lunches. The cafe is open 10.30am-4.30pm every weekday except Monday; Sunday noon-4.30pm.

Toilets including for the disabled. No nappy-changing facilities. Lift to upper floor and easy access into building.

HEALEY DELL NATURE TRAIL

Unit 34, Healey Hall Mills, Shawclough, Rochdale, OL12 6BG Tel: 01706 350459

A671 Rochdale-Bacup road. From Rochdale look for Station Road, a left turn off Whitworth Road. Follow this to Broadley Wood Lodge past the station, where there is car parking. Or follow direction above for Falinge Park for the Shaw Clough Road entrance. Difficult to find but signposting improving. For visitor centre B6377 opposite Healey Hotel.

Open daily.

Free car parking.

Free admission.

The visitor centre is sited at Healey Hall Mills where wardens are based, but it is out of the way. It is open most days between 1pm and 4pm and has an exhibition area. Wardens will chat to visitors and provide tea and coffee. Toilets are upstairs – no nappy changing or disabled facilities. School parties welcome by arrangement.

Healey Dell is well worth a visit all year round, but especially in spring and autumn when nature is at her best. The disused railway track goes over a viaduct from where there are wonderful views and there is a lovely walk back through the gorge taking a comfortable hour.

The woodland is oak, birch and beech, there is the Dell waterfall and the Fairies Chapel – strange rock shapes – to enjoy and plenty of wild life.

For pushchairs and wheelchairs there is good access, but only along the disused railway. People with limited mobility might find the walk through the gorge difficult. Wardens are working on an extended disabled route. Make sure you get an up-to-date trail guide to help plan your walk.

UNDER FIVES STORYTIME

Metro Rochdale Community Leisure Services. Tel: 01706 47474

Rochdale libraries.

Alkrington Library – Monday 2.30; Wheatsheaf Library- Monday 2.15; Heywood Library* – Tuesday 2.30; Spotland Library – Thursday 2.30; Middleton Library* – Thursdays 2.30; Littleborough Library* – Fridays 2.30. (*coffee is served at these venues.)

No, this isn't a day out but we've included this because it is rare to find something specifically for the under fives – and this is an excellent scheme.

Storytime happens at the above times at the above libraries. Mums, dads, grandparents are invited to stay and encouraged to sit apart from their toddler if possible. In some of the libraries coffee is served.

Stories and rhymes last about 20 minutes and then there is a craft activity, related to the story – making a hat, a butterfly, or a picture to colour. Babies come along too and there are board books to entertain them. Families usually finish by choosing their books to take home.

Most of these libraries also offer a storytime for four to 11-year-olds during the school holidays.

Choose your nearest library and check with them for other details.

WHEATSHEAF SHOPPING CENTRE

Penn Street, Rochdale.

Follow signs to town centre and Wheatsheaf shopping centre; situated near bus station in Rochdale town centre.

Open six days a week for shopping.

Car parking above centre or in bus station car park with walkways to shops.

Free admission.

You can shop in pleasant malls which are super for pushchairs and wheelchairs but it must have been designed by a man who has never been in charge of a pushchair – a flight of stairs greets you and your pushchair at the main entrance. A wheelchair lift has been installed here and there is a scenic lift, but other mums tell me you have to wait a long time – especially when it's busy. There is a soft enclosed play area for small children, unsupervised but open from 9am-5.30pm so youngsters can let off steam after shopping. Nearby is a fascinating working model of the South Georgia railways with trains, boats etc.

The Cotton Quay restaurant is self-service with hot meals and salads, has highchairs, boxed meals for children and children's parties catered for.

Toilets: disabled toilet with Radar key; good nappy-changing room with pushchair access, toilet and breastfeeding cubicle.

46

WHEATSHEAF LIBRARY

Baille Street, Rochdale.

This is located on the upper mall shopping level of the Wheatsheaf Shopping Centre (see above.) Direct access from bus station and bus station car parks via covered bridges.

Car parking in bus station car park.

Admission free.

Open Monday 9.30am-7.30pm; Tues to Fri inc. 9.30am-5.30pm; Sat 9.30am-5pm.

Services for visual or hearing impaired people close at 5pm Monday to Saturday.

This is a new library for Rochdale on three levels with stairs and lifts linking each floor. There are services for special groups on one level, and the main level houses the lending and children's libraries and a browsing area. The upper floor is for reference. The ethos of the place is a family library so it is very child-friendly. The children's area has animal floor cushions, kinder boxes holding books and there is a "large book" in which the librarian sits when reading to children. There are story times and activities for older children during every school holiday which may include puppets, crafts, entertainers and competitions – all with a book theme. A new and separate teenage department offers books for 11-14 year olds and 14 years upwards, with comfy seating and good paperbacks.

Ask for the key to the toilets which include disabled and a nappy changing room.

ESPLANADE ARTS AND HERITAGE CENTRE

Esplanade, Rochdale Gallery. Tel: 01706 342154.

Local studies 01706-864915; Museum 01706-41085.

M62, junction 20, follow signs to town centre. The Esplanade is where Rochdale's town hall is situated.

Town centre car parking, some short stay and long stay for disabled directly outside building.

Admission free

Please check opening times (Rochdale Tourist Information 01706-356592).

The former library and art gallery premises are being converted at a cost of £1 million into an arts and heritage centre housing the museum, the art gallery and the local studies gallery.

It is expected to be completed by the end of 1995, but areas are still being used and are open to the public. A rather posh leaflet describes all this using arty language – but it seems as though the people doing the work are down to earth and have the family at the centre of things. They hope to provide everything for families, from pushchair access, to nappy changing and feeding facilities, carefully thought-out toilets, cafe with children's food, and no doubt they'd be glad to have input from the town's people. Disabled people will be expertly catered for too. But apart from the basic facilities, it sounds as though there will be plenty to do and see, calling on Rochdale's history – not to mention Gracie Fields, the Co-operative Movement, the canal and its links with the textile industry.

A few minutes walk away, almost opposite the Town Hall, is a small park with a play area for children.

ROCHDALE PIONEERS MUSEUM

Toad Lane, Rochdale . Tel: 01706 524920

At rear of Rochdale Shopping Precinct, on Hunters Lane. Twelve minutes walk from Rochdale Railway Station and five minutes walk from bus station. Signposted for pedestrians from shopping precinct.

Open Tuesday to Saturday 10am-4pm; Sundays 2pm-4pm. Closed all day Monday. However, doors are locked 45 minutes before closing time.

Admission: adults 50p, children 10p. No charge for senior citizens.

Car parking in town centre; disabled car park in Hunters Lane.

The museum is regarded as the home of the world-wide Co-operative Movement because it is the original little store opened by the famous Rochdale Equitable Pioneers Society on December 21, 1844. This is a small but fascinating museum on two floors and particularly popular with school children and senior citizens. You can see the original shop with rudimentary furniture and scales. The museum houses documents and artefacts telling the story of the Pioneers and the Blue Peter pictures showing the development of the movement.

School parties are welcome and a guide tells the co-operative story. For bookings telephone 0161-832-4300. The visit is often coupled with a trip round Rochdale Town Hall (see below).

Access by wheelchair to ground floor only. Pushchairs could be carried upstairs. One toilet on first floor.

ROCHDALE TOWN HALL

Esplanade, Rochdale. Tel: 01706 47474 ext 4775

This is widely regarded as one of the finest Victorian Town Halls in the country with an impressive exterior and a richly decorated interior.

It is a working building and guided tours are by arrangement. Contact the Head Porter at the number above. The Town Hall and the Rochdale Pioneers Museum in Toad Lane are usually combined as tours for groups of schoolchildren or any age group.

HOLLINGWORTH LAKE AND COUNTRY PARK

Rakewood Road, Littleborough, Lancashire. Tel: 01706 373421
Signposted from Littleborough. Several car parks but make for the information centre car park if it is your first visit.
Information centre open seven days a week (closed Christmas Day.) Winter 10.30am-5pm; summer 10.30-7pm or 8pm.
Free admission.
Pay-and display parking at information centre.

There are several ways to enjoy Hollingworth Lake. One is to walk to a pleasant spot, sit and enjoy it – another is to walk round the lake. Trail guides available at the information centre. The two and a half mile walk is on the flat and fairly easy for pushchairs. But gravel paths, bumps and mud make things difficult for wheelchairs. First part of the trail follows Rakewood Road which is dangerous and narrow, with no footpaths, but then cars are left behind and the walking is enjoyable. The trail passes a play area for very small children, just off the road, and a playground for older children including a wooden boat to climb on. Dog dirt can be a problem but poop scoop bins are now situated round the lake.

At the Sailing Club (see below) boats are for hire and seats available on a large pleasure boat for a sail round the lake. Nearby is a large pub which caters for families, a small cafe with one highchair, welcomes children. A small amusement arcade is nearby, suitable for older children.

Many children paddle at the water's edge and some actually swim in the water although it does not look clean. Be prepared to say "no" or take plastic shoes, buckets, spades etc.

Information centre houses displays about the history of the lake and its wildlife. Shop selling souvenir items. Cafe (no highchairs as yet) but will heat up baby food and bottles. Toilets, including disabled people; nappy-changing facilities.

At the bottom of the car park near the visitor centre there is a pond, large grassed area and picnic tables.

50

WATER ACTIVITY CENTRE

The Boat House, Lake Bank, Littleborough OL15 0DQ . Tel: 01706 370499

Follow signs from Littleborough to Hollingworth Lake. The boat house is at lakeside away from information centre.

Courses in sailing, windsurfing, canoeing and rowing for children in the Splashout Club. Age groups 7-9,10-12,13-15. Mini Splashout 4-6 year olds (sailing only). Courses are run on a four-day basis. Also courses available for older children, adults, school groups, special needs groups.

All run under the auspices of Metro Rochdale.

THREE OWLS BIRD SANCTUARY AND RESERVE

Wolstenholme Fold, Norden, Rochdale, OL11 5UD. Tel: 01706 42162

From Rochdale take the Spotland Road (A680) to Edenfield and Blackburn; on reaching Norden village, look for church spire on right – a little further is the bus terminus on the left; turn left here at Hutchinson Road; keep going past the park and on an unmade road; sanctuary on left.

Open Sundays 2pm-5pm and Bank Holidays for visitors or by appointment; for casualties 9am-6pm Monday to Saturday.

Free admission – donations extremely welcome.

Car parking very difficult for more than half a dozen cars.

Mrs Eileen Watkinson first took in an abandoned baby sparrow one night in 1962. To her surprise it lived – and the bird sanctuary was born. The property and grounds now housing the sanctuary was loaned to Mrs Watkinson in 1970 and it is hoped they can be bought to ensure its future. Spring and early summer are the busiest time for casualties and the bird hospital looks after its patients 24 hours a day.

This is a small, muddy place with plenty of puddles and there is definitely no access for pushchairs or wheelchairs! Even an arthritic granny with a stick would have difficulty. Take wellies for your children in the winter.

It is however a worthwhile project and young children will learn a lot – not least about the bad treatment some adults and children give to birds but also the wonderful care some other adults give. The case of each individual bird is fascinating. Those that can be are returned to the wild. Depending on what's there at the time, you will see owls, crows, ravens, heron, ducks, geese, kestrels, seagulls ...

Donations are desperately needed for the food bill and more; you can adopt a bird, or become a friend of Three Owls.

Visitors are given a guided tour, but it can be a little haphazard.

There is a toilet and a vending machine. In summer teas are served from a cottage round the corner.

THE MANOR – CHARLIE CHALK FUN FACTORY

Edenfield Road, Norden, Rochdale, OL12 7TW. Tel: 01706-50027.
A680 between Rochdale and Edenfield at Norden.
Open Monday to Saturday 11.30am-10pm, Sundays noon-10pm.
Free car parking.
Free admission.

This is a large, imposing pub set in its own grounds, owned by Brewer's Fayre. There is a sincere family welcome here and the accent is on fun and food rather than drink.

Inside the pub there is the "fun factory" which has soft play facilities for under fives and under eights. There are ball pools, things to climb on and roll about in – all great fun and mum and dad can sit nearby with a drink. It is difficult to supervise very small children as there is not much room for spectators. But parents of older children can sit in the adjoining bar. Outside there are two soft surfaced play areas, one for four to eight-year-olds and the other up to a maximum of 14 years. Also bouncy castle. There are tables and chairs for parents. The only thing they frown on is pushchairs in the pub – because of the fire risk. And pleasant notices ask you to comply with this rule.

The pub has lots of highchairs, there is a microwave in the baby changing room for you to heat up bottles (key from the bar). Children's menu is the usual "....with chips", modestly priced. Lots of adult meals including vegetarian dishes and dishes of the day.

Toilets, nappy-changing and feeding room, toilets for disabled people.

COUNTRYSIDE EVENTS

Tel: 01706 373421

Countryside Rangers in the Rochdale area provide a calendar of events throughout the year, some of which are ideal for young families. The events are held at or start from such places as Hollingworth Lake Visitor Centre (see above), Trap Farm car park at Wardle, Healey

Dell (see above), Alkrington Wood at Middleton and Hopwood College, Middleton. Most are on Sundays but some are held on other days.

Activities specifically for children are held fortnightly on Saturday afternoons at the Visitor Centre, Hollingworth Lake. Wardens are also keen to help with schools.

The leaflets giving details of the events offer a small map for car drivers and bus numbers for those using public transport.

CHORLEY

ALL SEASONS LEISURE CENTRE SWIMMING POOL

Water Street, Chorley, PR7 1EX . Tel: 01257 267921

M61, junction 7, then A6 to Chorley. From north: M6, junction 29, then the A6 into Chorley. From south: M6, junction 27, then A49 for Chorley. Within five minutes walk of Chorley town hall off dual carriageway at Water Street; signposted.

Open Monday to Friday 8am-8pm; Saturday and Sunday 8am-4pm.

Free car park.

Adults £1.75, children £1.25, OAPs £1.25, under fives free – for one-hour swim.

The swimming pool opened in September 1991 and has every modern facility. There is a 25 metre pool for serious swimmers and a 10 metre learner pool heated to about 86 degrees F, so perfect for babies and non-swimmers with shallow, sloped areas. Warm bubble pool and water slide for small children adds to the fun. Changing rooms have curtained cubicles with three family cubicles in the women's and two in the men's. These are simply larger curtained cubicles for parents and two or more children. Baby changing tables.

Mum and baby sessions – check times. No access to poolside for pushchairs. Building designed with disabled in mind with ramps, lift and easy access including lift to help disabled swimmers into the pool available at all times.

There are also squash courts, a sports hall, fitness suite and bar on the site. Creche also available Mon-Fri 10am-noon.

No cafe – vending machines only. Two areas of poolside seating. Toilets with disabled and nappy changing facilities. No baby feeding facilities.

ASTLEY HALL AND PARK AND THE STABLES CAFE

Astley Park, Chorley, Lancs, PR7 1DP . Tel: 01257 262166

Park is reached within a few minutes walk of Chorley Town Hall. By car M6, junction 28, A49/A581 Southport Road and pick up signs to hall. M61, junction 8, A6 Chorley and B5252 – follow signs for Astley Village.

Open April-end October daily 11am-noon and 1pm-5pm. From November 1- end March only open on Friday, Saturday and Sunday (and Easter Monday) 11am-noon and 1pm-4pm. Closed December 25 to January 2 inclusive.

Free car parking.

Admission to hall, adult £2, children £1, under fives free; family tickets (two adults, two children £4.). Free to disabled children. Admission to park free.

The hall offers the visitor the experience of an English country house during the Late Tudor and Early Stuart England period of history (1580-1650). Only the downstairs is accessible by pushchair or wheelchair and as it is a listed building, ramps and lifts cannot be installed. Children are welcome to walk round with parents.

The hall is set in 105 acres of parkland with woodland walks, an ornamental pond with ducks, putting, tennis and bowls. Across a bridge from the house is a large fenced area with goats, rabbits and etc., and nearby is a children's play area suitable for small children with only one baby swing.

Dogs are allowed in the park but owners must clean up after them – or be fined.

The Stables Cafe opens every day except Christmas Day and Boxing Day; summer – 10am-5pm, winter – 11am-3pm. This is a family cafe where children are welcome. Hot and cold food, children's dishes like fish finger and chips; non-fizzy drinks, will heat up babies' bottles, highchairs. Toilets, including for the disabled and nappy changing facilities.

Adjacent to the car park is the Inn on the Park (01257 260712). Sunday lunches are served in the restaurant and there are highchairs. Bar snacks available in the bar all year round noon-2pm and afternoon teas. Well behaved children are welcome. During the summer the bar serves pop, crisps and ice-cream for children. Also afternoon teas. Beer garden for summer months but no play equipment.

Toilets at the inn, including for the disabled; no nappy-changing facilities.

CAMELOT THEME PARK

Charnock Richard, Chorley, near Preston, Lancashire, PR7 5LP. Tel: 01257-453044

Short drive from M6 (junction 27 northbound and junction 28 southbound) or M61 junction 8. Well signposted.

Open daily April to September 10am-6pm.

Well-ordered free parking with flat access to main gate. Disabled parking.

Admission: adults and children £9.99, OAP and disabled £4.75. Groups of 12 or more £4.75. Under fours free.

The theme park is geared for the four to 14-year-olds but there are plenty of things to suit younger children too. An undercover area with child activity centre, slides and a ball pool keep under fives happy for a long time. There are rides suitable for under fives but adults are not allowed on some, so children have to be confident enough to go alone. Family rides for parents and children together. More than 100 rides and attractions, many under cover, but be prepared to queue for the most popular ones at busy times. Lots of live shows and entertainment throughout the day.

Plenty of eating places but most sell "fast food." Picnic areas and plenty of grass to sit on. Cafes do have highchairs and children's menus.

Lots of toilets, including for disabled people and nappy changing facilities. Breast feeders welcome in either of the two first aid offices.

Paths are well maintained and easy for pushchairs and wheelchairs with ramps and gangways – although the site does have a couple of hills.

BOLTON

BUTTERFLY WORLD AND QUEENS PARK

Chorley New Road, Bolton . Tel: 01204 363528

From Bolton town centre, follow signs to the A673 Chorley New Road, signposted M61. From M61, exit 5: follow dual carriageway and then left along ring road, until sign for A673. Signpost to Butterfly World very small if coming from motorway, large if from town centre.

Open 10am-5pm daily April to October; noon-4pm November; December to March closed, but check as times alter.

Free admission to park; Butterfly World costs £1.40 adults; children 5-16 years 65p; under fives free; pensioners and disabled people 70p. Family ticket for two adults and two children £3.45.

Free parking on Chorley New Road; a short walk to the park.

Butterfly World is a renovated conservatory in Queens Park which is filled with exotic plants and the home of dozens of marvellous

butterflies and moths in free flight. The conservatory is small, but you can spend some time in there, observing the butterflies and although you are not allowed to touch them, you can stand still and hope one alights on you! There are also some scorpions, large spiders. locusts and grasshoppers in tanks as well as a pool with goldfish. It is very hot (80F) so dress in layers and be prepared to carry coats.

There's a small gift shop and indoor picnic area where teas and coffees are available, but you can eat your own food.

Access throughout for wheelchairs and pushchairs but not much room. Toilets, including for the disabled, in the park; key available from Butterfly World.

The park itself is large and pleasant, with a children's playground, containing two baby swings, slide, roundabout, see-saw etc and plenty of soft surfaces. There's a duck pond too.

THE WATER PLACE

Great Moor Street, Bolton, BL1 1SP. Tel: 01204 364616

Well signposted on all approaches to Bolton and is located in Bolton town centre, next to Morrison's supermarket. Short walk from bus station.

Opening hours vary and there are sometimes special sessions so check first.

Admission: Monday to Friday, adults £2, children £1.65. After 6pm and at weekends, adult £2.75, children £2.10.

Car parking either short stay (2 hours) off Great Moor Street, or long-stay in the nearby multi-storey. A special six-place disabled parking area for badge-holding visitors to the Water Place is off Dawes Road.

Forget your standard pool – this is an experience. Aquaflumes, wild water channel, raging river ride, tidal wave, bubble beds and spa pool all make for a "simply splashing" time. There is a gentle "beach" area with children's elephant slide especially for under fives although there are other areas they could enjoy too. Plenty of foliage for atmosphere and lots of lifeguards for safety. There's also a trainer pool with lane ropes and under-water music.

There are communal changing rooms, baby changing tables, family changing rooms and pushchair access near to the children's play-pool. Kinderswim usually Tuesday and Thursday 10.30am-noon and there are sometimes swimming lessons for three to five-year-olds. Can be hired for parties. Everywhere is accessible on wheels with ramps to all levels but pushchairs not allowed on pool side. There's a hoist to lift disabled swimmers into the water – simply ask when you arrive.

The cafe is fairly basic – chips, sandwiches, drinks etc – but has highchairs and is friendly and there is a poolside view.

Toilets including for the disabled and nappy changing facilities.

Opposite main doors is Morrison's supermarket; their restaurant has highchairs, children's specials, baby food available and they will heat up yours; open Monday, Tuesday Saturday 8am-6.30pm, Wednesday, Thursday, Friday 8am-8pm. Toilets with pushchair access but no nappy-changing facility.

BOLTON CENTRAL MUSEUM, ART GALLERY, AQUARIUM AND LIBRARY

Le Mans Crescent, Bolton, BL1 1SE. Tel: 01204 22311 ext 2191

In the town centre near the town hall and the Albert Halls.

Lending library open Monday, Tuesday, Thursday, Friday 9.30-7.30; Wednesday 9.30am-1pm,Saturday 9.30am-5pm. Museum Monday, Tuesday, Thursday, Friday 9.30am-5.30pm, Saturday 10am-5pm, closed Wednesday and Sunday.

Admission free.

Parking in one of town centre car parks.

All these facilities are housed in one large and imposing building. The museum and art gallery doesn't have much to interest the under fives but they may enjoy the natural history section which is (unfortunately) up a large flight of stairs (see below) and older children will enjoy the Egyptology collection. There are worksheets and quizzes for young visitors. School parties are welcome by appointment.

In the basement there is an aquarium with freshwater and marine fish in large tanks which are not set too high for little ones. But the aquarium is reached by a flight of about seven steps.

The library has a children's library. Activities for children are staged in both the museum and the library during the summer holidays.

Pushchairs and wheelchairs can use the ramp to get to the ground floor and from there, there is a passenger lift. It is possible to get to the natural history section via a service lift if you ask but there are further steps to the aquarium.

New toilets in basement with toilet for disabled people. No nappy-changing facilities.

SMITHILLS HALL MUSEUM

Off Smithills Dean Road, Bolton. Tel: 01204 841265

Signposted of the A58 two miles north west of Bolton.

Open April to September; Tuesday to Saturday 11am-5pm. Sunday 2pm-5pm. Closed October to March inclusive.

Admission from £1.55 adults. Dual ticket may be bought for entry here and to Hall I'th' Wood (see below).

Car parking.

This is one of the oldest and most attractively situated manor houses in Lancashire. The oldest part of the house is the 14th century Great Hall. Access for wheels to ground floor only.

Pleasant grounds and gardens make it a good family day out and there is a nature trail. Toilets, but not for disabled people and no nappy-changing facility.

SMITHILLS COACHING HOUSE just off Smithills Dean Road (01204 840377) is a child-friendly family restaurant, open lunchtime and evenings during the week and all day Saturday and Sunday. There is an extensive children's menu plus a Sunday roast dinner for children at £2.99. Under twos can have soup and ice-cream free. Highchairs. Toilets, including male and female disabled; nappy-changing facilities.

Also nearby is SMITHILLS GARDEN CENTRE which has a small children's play area, welcomes families and has toilet facilities.

HALL I'TH' WOOD

Green Way, off Crompton Way, Bolton BL1 8UA. Tel: 01204 301159
Signposted off the A58 north of Bolton.
Open April to September, Tuesday to Saturday 11am-5pm; Sunday 2pm-5pm.
Admission from £1.55 for adults; dual ticket available for here and Smithills Hall
(see above).
Car parking.

This is a late medieval merchant's house with striking black and white exterior. It was the home of Samuel Crompton when he was five until he was about 29 and it was here he invented the Spinning Mule in 1779. Many people visit both this and Smithills Hall on a visit to Bolton. This is the smaller of the two and access only to ground floor with wheels. Grounds and outside toilets, but not for disabled people.

Hall i'th'Wood may be closed for a year or more from late 1994 for extensive restoration work, so please check before visiting.

BOLTON – SHOPPING AND CHILDREN'S ENTERTAINMENT

Extremely good shopping town centre, mainly on the level with pedestrian-only areas and the award-winning Market Hall which has a Radar key toilet for disabled people and nappy-changing facilities. Mothercare on Market Street near the town hall has a mother and baby room in the basement, reached by a lift. British Home Stores has a nappy-changing facility in the ladies' toilets, but this is also in the basement (there is a lift) and along a long corridor and up three difficult steps if you have a pushchair. The Bus Station also has a Radar key toilet for disabled people. Disabled parking located around the town hall and in most car parks.

The Albert Halls present children's entertainment every so often; check with the booking and tourist information office in the Albert Halls (01204 22311).

MOSS BANK PARK

A66 to Blackburn from Bolton, left into Halliwell Road, left again into Moss Bank Way and into park on right at second set of lights. Three or four miles from town centre.

Open daily.

Free admission.

Free car park.

This is a large, pleasant park with wide pathways and easy access for wheelchairs and pushchairs. Lots of grass for ball games, but lots of dogs too. The children's play area is a little disappointing, although it has six baby swings! A large enclosed sandpit (no dogs allowed) can be fun. Great miniature railway for children which operates in the summer and at weekends, depending on the weather. Also boat swings (40p per ride) which operate seasonally.

The park has a good pet's corner and aviary – see rabbits, peacocks, guinea pigs, ducks etc., along with a python, tree frogs, chipmunks, iguanas, and small exotic birds. Playcentre open for indoor activities for children – pool, paper and crayons – as well as use of outdoor equipment. Tennis, bowls, pitch and putt.

Park is host to local events including the final of "Holidays at Home" races during last week of local wakes – usually about second week in July.

Cafe open in summer and fine weekends.

Toilets near pets' corner; no nappy-changing facility; toilet for disabled people with Radar key.

LAST DROP VILLAGE

Hospital Road, Bromley Cross, Bolton . Tel: 01204 591131

Signposted from M61, junction 5, and from Bolton from the A676: about four miles from the town centre.

Open all year.

Car parking.

Free admission.

Although not really a day out, this has to be mentioned when covering the Bolton area. It is an 18th century farm, imaginatively converted and extended to provide a picturesque "village" complete with cottages, workshops, restaurant, cocktail bar, hotel, tea shop etc. You can visit the village and walk round, stop for lunch or whatever. We were assured children were welcome and highchairs are available.

The hotel has a pool and leisure complex. Families tend to stay at weekends (children free when sharing parents' room) and enjoy use of the leisure facilities. There is a dinner-dance every Saturday and an antiques fair every Sunday.

Wheelchair and pushchair access limited.

64

JUMBLES COUNTRY PARK AND INFORMATION CENTRE

Bradshaw Road, Bradshaw, Bolton . Tel: 01204 853360

Off A676 Bradshaw Road between Bolton and Ramsbottom.

Park open daily; information centre open in summer from 1pm-5pm Wednesday, Saturday; Sunday and Bank Holidays 10am-5pm. Winter Sundays only 11.30am-5pm.

Free admission.

Free car parking. Disabled parking with view near to information centre.

The Jumbles reservoir trail offers a pleasant and scenic walk round the reservoir which would take about an hour or more. Pushchair and wheelchair access only halfway – unless you have help to negotiate stiles and gates and a final 60-odd steps back to car park.

There is a self-guided nature trail, a bird hide which is baited in winter, benches and picnic tables all the way round and ducks to feed. The information centre has a display area, books and leaflets for sale and a small classroom for schoolchildren. School visits by appointment.

Jumbles gets very busy a certain times – expect the car park to be full on sunny Saturdays and Sundays.

Various guided walks with themes arranged, but wardens usually suggest only children over the age of six can manage summer walks; and older children on the winter rambles. Children must be properly equipped and no prams or pushchairs allowed. Countryside events programme throughout the year – leaflets available.

Toilets are in car park, including for disabled people with Radar key.

Jumbles tea garden serves cream teas, home made pastries etc in the outdoors – seating for about 50 people including picnic bench for wheelchair users.

From Jumbles, walkers can follow a ten-and-half-mile trail taking in the TURTON, ENTWISTLE AND WAYOH reservoir trails. These trails can also be circulars but Wayoh only accessible part of the way on wheels; Entwistle is passable part of the way round with wheels; no toilets.

RIVINGTON
& ANGLEZARKE

Rivington Lane, Rivington, Horwich, Bolton, BL6 7SB. Tel: 01204-691549

M61, junction 6, follow signs to Horwich then signs to great House Barn Information Centre at Rivington. BR stations at Blackrod and Adlington, one and a half miles; Hourly bus service operated by Timeline; GM buses only on Sundays in the season.

Free short-stay car parking for up to three hours at Great House Barn. Long stay for those who want to go on a day's walk at Hall Barn or Rivington Lane car park.

Free admission.

Barn open daily but not always staffed.

Rivington and Anglezarke are two reservoirs which lie on the south western edge of the West Pennine Moors. Much of the character of Rivington is owed to W.H.Lever, later to become Lord Leverhulme, who gave nearby Lever Park to the people of Bolton in 1902.

New visitors would do well to park at the Great Barn, ask for information and proceed from there. But briefly, you can walk by the reservoirs, stroll in the woodland, enjoy Rivington Hall and its terraced gardens, and walk up to Rivington Pike. There are local and natural history trails – Anglezarke Woodland Trail, Upper Rivington Reservoir Trail, Lead Mines Clough and Rivington Terraces Gardens trail.

Access to both reservoirs is possible with pushchairs and wheelchairs but not throughout. There is a disabled parking area at Anglezarke reservoir and quite good access for pushchairs and wheelchairs along much of the pathways. Plenty of places to picnic with picnic tables near all car parks.

Large cafe at Great Barn is open 11am-5pm every day serving snacks and meals; warm welcome for children from manageress who will go out of her way to give children what they want to eat as well as heating up bottles and baby food. Highchairs.

Toilets, including Radar toilets for disabled. Radar keys available at information shop. No nappy changing facilities.

TURTON HEIGHTS PUB AND JUNGLE BUNGLE

Bradshaw Road, Turton, Bolton, BL7 0HR. Tel: 01204-852475

Off the A676 Bradshaw Road at Turton Heights crossroads.

Car park, including slow-down ramps for access to car park near Jungle Bungle.

Admission to pub free; Jungle Bungle £1 for 45-55 minutes.

Pub open daily; Jungle Bungle noon-3pm and 6pm-9pm Monday to Friday; Saturday, Sunday and Bank Holidays noon-9pm.

Turton heights is a Miller's Kitchen pub with the accent on food rather than drink. The Jungle Bungle is housed in a pretty cottage type building at the rear and is a soft play area for children. They have tried very hard indeed to provide everything a family with children needs.

The restaurant area is comfortable and stylish and the special family area has bench seats around a table which would seat a family of six to eight. They sell Heinz baby foods, have a special menu for small children, plus one for junior diners. Senior citizens can also eat from this more modestly-priced menu. A full range of dishes for adult diners including a full vegetarian menu and dishes of the day. The family area has a video with cartoons and a small area with small table and chairs for little ones to play.

There is pushchair and wheelchair access, toilets including for the disabled and nappy changing facilities. (Although the latter facility is a pull-down from the wall kind, suitable only for small babies, not toddlers and is situated in the small, ladies' loo area. But should we complain when everything else is so well thought out?!)

The JUNGLE BUNGLE has a safe area for two-five year olds and the rest is for children up to the height of 4ft 9ins (probably no older than 10). There are ball pools, slides – all the fun of a soft play area. Children are given coloured tabards which denote the time they came in as it is strictly limited to 45-55 minutes at busy times. Adults can sit and watch children play. Drinks (in plastic cups) can be taken in. Tea, coffee, crisps, chocolates and ice creams are also available in the Jungle Bungle. It's available for private parties. Toilets and nappy changing facilities in here too.

HEYWOOD ADVENTURE PLAYWORLD

High Street, Great Lever, Bolton BL3 6SR. Tel: 01204-23408

Take the A579 to Leigh from Bolton and turn right along High Street.

Open all year outdoors. Indoors open 9am-6pm Monday to Friday although the facilities may be booked privately during this time. Weekends – private parties. After school play scheme during term time 4pm-6pm, school holidays open noon-6pm. Under fives centre 10am-noon. Please check times before setting out.

Admission – free outdoors, indoors 50p session of 1-2 hours depending how busy it is.

Owned by Bolton Metro, this is a wonderful place for children under 10 years with plenty to do to let off steam and get rid of excess energy. Outside there is a play area with safety surfaces which includes a toddler area, a junior high activity area, a 10-plus area, an assault course, a picnic area and a musical sensory garden. Outside toilets with nappy changing facilities. Inside is a wonderful soft play area for children but it is very popular. Only 30 children at a time, so first come first served – but they do limit time to one hour at very busy times. You can leave your child alone here if it is over five years. At the under fives centre parents must stay and there are morning and some afternoon sessions.

Teas and coffees are served indoors for parents. Ice cream van outside. But you can take a picnic and your own drinks.

STOCKPORT
and parts of Cheshire

LYME PARK

Disley, Stockport SK12 2NX . Tel: 01663 762023

Only vehicular entrance on the Manchester to Buxton A6 road, half a mile west of Disley village. Regular bus services from Stockport to Disley.

Park open all year 8am-8.30pm or dusk if earlier. Opening times vary for Hall, National Trust Information Centre, Gardens and refreshment kiosk, so please check.

National Trust members free, family ticket £6.25, hall and garden adult £2.50, garden only adult £1, park per car £3. Concessions for children and others.

Lyme is a National Trust property. More than 1,300 acres of deerpark with wild moorland scenery where red deer have roamed for centuries plus, the orangery and 16 acres of formal Victorian gardens.

The hall is reached up a steep hill or steps; battery-powered scooter for older or disabled people available. The home of the Legh family for 600 years, the hall has interiors from various periods of history, as well as English furniture, family portraits and a collection of clocks. A written children's guide is available. No pushchairs, no children in backpacks. Grand staircase to long gallery. Access for disabled people is limited but if you telephone in advance, every help will be offered. Some parts of the garden and park can be reached by wheelchair.

Enclosed adventure playground – no dogs. Picnic area within playground. Large duck pond in the park and another picnic area nearby.

Tea room with highchair, shop, both accessible to wheelchairs Refreshment kiosk open at June, July and weekends. (Little Chef on A6 east of Disley)

Toilets including for disabled people.

ETHEROW COUNTRY PARK

George Street, Compstall, Stockport. SK6 5JD. Tel: 0161 427 6937
At Compsall on the B6104 between Romiley and Marple Bridge. Signposted from the road.
Open seven days a week throughout the year. Visitor Centre closed Christmas Day.
Free admission.
Car parking 50p. Also pay-and-display near library and free car parking nearby.

Etherow Country Park was one of Britain's first country parks, established in 1968 around an old cotton mill. It now attracts more than a quarter of a million visitors a year, so expect lots of people on good days. There is a large lake, the river Etherow, a weir and woodland walks.

The many varieties of ducks and geese meet you as soon as you get out of the car which can be daunting for little children although it makes great entertainment for older ones. Take bread to feed them or buy a 20p bag of corn from the visitor centre which is better for them (and the profits go to buying more species.)

There are several paths to take. The simplest is a walk around the water on flat, wide and even paths, ideal for pushchairs and wheelchairs. It took us an hour with lots of loitering.

The whole of the park, including Keg Woods, is possible on wheels, but more difficult, and would take about three hours.

But there are picnic spots, places to play and if you buy the visitors' guide, lots to look out for.

There is a Coal Trail through Erncroft Wood which follows the history of coal mining in the area. A leaflet gives details. The route is steep in places and may be difficult for pushchairs.

Model boat enthusiasts also use the lake. There is a Braille-Trail with a tape and earphones to be borrowed from the visitor centre. They also have two electric wheelchairs and one manual for free hire.

Extra activities happen during the school holidays and there is a winter events leaflet – but most of these are for adults.

The visitor centre has some fun things for children, all at child level and this is where you ought to get a leaflet before you set off.

A holiday home which sleeps up to eight people is available for rent and a new one is being built, especially for disabled people. Contact the visitor centre for details of bookings.

The cafe opens all year, sometimes up to 9pm in summer and 4.30pm in winter. No highchairs.

Toilets including a disabled cubicle – access round the back of the visitor centre. Large table in ladies makes possible nappy-changing area. Toilets also at the weir (refer to map).

THE ETHEROW VALLEY WAY is an attractive 11-mile way-marked walk from the centre of Stockport to Hollingworth near Glossop, following the course of the river. Guide book (50p) available from the Etherow Goyt Valley Warden Service (0161-427-6937). Stout footwear is necessary and discuss the route with the warden service if you are not sure about your children's abilities.

STOCKPORT MUSEUM, VERNON AND WOODBANK PARKS

Vernon Park, Turncroft Lane, Offerton, SK1 4AR. Tel: 0161-474-4460

Approached off the A560, New Zealand Road and Turncroft Lane. For buses, ring BUSLINE on 01298 23098.

Parks open all year. Museum open every day April to October, 1-5pm. Winter opening Saturday and Sunday only, 1-5pm.

Free admission.

Car parks off Turncroft Lane.

Vernon Park was once a formal park, now less so; two bowling greens. Woodbank Park has football and cricket pitches, toilets. The play-ground has the usual swings and things with soft surfaces.

The museum covers the social and industrial history of the neigh-bourhood from the early cave dwellers to modern times, including the Romans, Anglo-Saxons, 1066 and all that. There is also a display of domestic appliances and toys up to about 1960. As Stockport is the centre of the hat making industry, there is a fascinating display of hatting, with its history and some miniature hats to see. Interesting for mums, dads and grandparents and with some small interest for the very young. School parties by appointment. Activities for children in school holidays – please check for details.

Difficult access for both wheelchairs and pushchairs. There are 26 steps to the upper floor – possible if two of you carry the pushchair, but impossible for the severely disabled.

Cafe selling teas, coffees etc open when museum is open.

Thirteen steps to toilets in basement. Disabled facilities applied for. No nappy changing facilities.

THE GOYT WAY

This is a 10-mile route which follows the valley of the River Goyt between Etherow Country Park, Compsall and Whaley Bridge.

It is waymarked with a logo shown on the leaflet available. The route has been chosen with easy access in mind and is well served by car parks and public transport. You can walk all or part of the route or take trains one way and walk the other. Most of the walking is easy but good shoes or boots are advisable.

We wouldn't recommend it with pushchair or wheelchair. Take babies in a back-pack if you feel strong enough and if older ones are capable of such a long walk.

The Goyt Way now links with the Midshires Way, which is a long distance footpath going through Brinnington and on to Stockport. A package of leaflets is available from Etherow and other locations, which gives details of the walk. It is signposted with the symbol M and two acorns.

To see if it would suit your family, check with the warden service at Etherow Country Park on 0161-427-6937 and get hold of the specially printed blue leaflet, The Goyt Way.

For details of buses ring BUSLINE 01298 23098 or GMPTE 0161-228-7811. For trains ring British Rail on 0161-832-8353.

REDDISH VALE CYCLE RIDE

For further details contact the Cycling Project for the North West, Environmental Institute, Bolton Road, Swinton, Manchester, M27 2UX . Tel: 0161 794 1926

This is a five mile cycle ride starting at Sainsbury's Supermarket in Stockport and wandering along the banks of the River Tame, along a disused railway line and then to Reddish Vale Visitor Centre.

It is for inexperienced cyclists or family groups. Most of this route is on paths, which may in places be muddy or bumpy. A few barriers exist to deter motorbikes. You may need to dismount.

Before you leave pump up your tyres hard. Look out for other vehicles, horses, dogs, joggers, walkers and prams!

Families with keen young cyclists may well tackle this cycle ride; baby seats are available at cycle shops to accommodate the very young.

The ride starts or ends at Reddish Vale Visitor Centre where there are toilets, but only cold drinks on sale. It is worth dismounting here and having a look at the Centre (see below).

REDDISH VALE VISITOR CENTRE

Reddish Vale Road, Mill Lane, Reddish, Stockport. Tel: 0161-477-5637

Signposted off the B6167 from Stockport, called Reddish Road. Ten minutes drive from Stockport town centre.

Open May to September, Monday and Wednesday 11am-4pm, Saturday and Sunday 10am-5pm. Winter, Monday and Wednesday 11am-3pm, Saturday and Sunday 10am-4pm.

Free admission.

Free parking.

The centre houses a permanent exhibition on the Tame Valley and temporary exhibition on the countryside. It is very child-friendly with touch tables, crawly tunnel, feely tables, fish tanks at child height and so on. It's a single storey building with access for pushchairs and wheelchairs.

There is a trail of 20-30 minutes suitable for wheelchairs and pushchairs and raised flower beds at the centre for disabled people to enjoy. There are picnic sites and a playfield for ball games. Horse riding and day ticket fishing ponds nearby.

Cartons of cold drinks available but no other refreshments unless mobile cafe turns up.

There's a list of free activities both summer and winter at the centre, many for families. Ask for leaflet. Toilets including for the disabled; no nappy-changing facilities.

MIDDLEWOOD WAY

For leaflets about the walk call at Macclesfield Tourist Information, Town Hall, Market Place (01625-421955), or pick one up at Poynton Information Centre and local libraries and cafes.

An 11-mile route from Macclesfield to Marple. Part of the area is managed by Macclesfield Borough Council's Leisure Services who employ a small team of countryside rangers. They operate from Adlington Road, Bollington (01625 573998). Macclesfield Borough Council has spent a great deal of energy and money developing the Way as a leisure route and it continues to do so.

North of Middlewood, the Way continues on to Rose Hill Station in Marple. Here the Way is managed by the Etherow-Goyt Wardens (0161-427-6937).

Bollington can be reached from the A537 Macclesfield to Stockport road. By train – there are British Rail stations at Marple, Middlewood, Adlington (about one mile away) and Macclesfield. BR – 0161-832-8353. Bus services run close to the Middlewood Way: ring 01625 534850.

Car parks at Rose Hill Station, Marple, High Lane, Higher Poynton, Bollington and Macclesfield. If parking at Rose Hill Station car park, Marple, don't walk along the track: go back onto the road, through the council yard to the footpath.

This is a lovely, traffic-free route for 11 miles for you to walk, ride a horse or cycle along. It is a former railway line bought by Macclesfield Borough Council. Improvements and changes are taking place all the time. The Macclesfield Canal runs almost parallel to the Way and several public footpaths link with Middlewood Way.

For young families it is rather too far to walk the whole length but from Bollington to Higher Poynton – about four miles – is a popular route and distance.

The way is almost accessible for pushchairs but gates to deter motor bikes can make access difficult if not impossible. But there is disabled access onto the canal towpath south of Bollington, but best check the leaflet and with the rangers first.

There is a suitable path for horses on the Way with limited facilities for parking horse boxes at Higher Poynton and Bollington. Cyclists are being asked to use the horse track rather than the footpath for the safety of walkers.

Wildlife is encouraged in the area and there are walks and talks organised by the rangers. (contact them on the phone number above.) There are picnic sites along the way. The Boar's Head at Poynton does pub lunches, there's the Miner's Arms at Wood Lane, Ken's Cafe nearby which serves hot food and there are cafes and sweet shops at Higher Poynton.

Toilets at Higher Poynton Station and Poynton Marina: Radar key operated toilets for disabled people at Adlington Road, Bollington.

No nappy-changing facilities.

NEW HORIZONS – STOCKPORT CANAL TRUST FOR HANDICAPPED PEOPLE

Booking Centre (please send an SAE): Mr Warwick Royle, 2, Fishers Bridge, Hayfield, Stockport, Cheshire, SK12 5JZ. Tel: 01663-742796

The Stockport Canal Trust for Handicapped People was created by a former mayor of Stockport whose charity appeal was to raise money to build the specially designed narrowboat " New Horizons." The boat was commissioned by H.R.H. The Prince of Wales in 1981. The idea is to provide holidays on the canals of the northwest for handicapped and disabled people for a half or whole day, or as long as a week.

The boat is usually moored at Marple in Cheshire and trips of one day for up to 12 people or one week for up to eight people can be booked. But it's recommended that the number of people confined to wheelchairs should be no more than six. It can be hired by any individual, family or group with disabled members. There is even a facility for people on dialysis.

The boat has specially fitted toilet, shower and eating facilities and a lift enables passengers to reach the raised fore-deck, giving wonderful views over the countryside. Two raisable bunks enable prone passengers to see out. The boat has all mod cons, including television, mobile telephone and heating.

For day trips, passengers own food can be taken or the boat will call at one of the canal side pubs on the way where the landlord welcomes disabled people. A skipper and crewman go with each party.

Being a charity, they are always short of funds – so if you feel like helping handicapped people have a Great Day Out, you can send money to Mr Royle at the address above.

BURY

EAST LANCASHIRE RAILWAY

Bolton Street, Bury, Lancashire BL9 0EY. Tel 0161-764-7790 weekends;
0161-705-5111 weekdays

M62, junction 18, take M66 to Bury. M66, junction 3. Regular bus services from
Manchester and surrounding towns to Bury and Ramsbottom. A frequent electric
train service operates between Manchester (Victoria Station) and Bury on all days
except Sunday.

Open Saturdays, Sundays and Bank Holidays: telephone for details or collect a
timetable from tourist information centres. (Bury Tourist Information, Market Street,
0161-705-5111).

Car parking in Bury town centre and parking at Ramsbottom, Summerseat and
Rawtenstall.

Fares (1994) – Bury to Rawtenstall adult return £5, child return £3. Children under
five free. Other fares available as well as singles.

This is an attractive steam and diesel train service running from Bury
to Rawtenstall along the Irwell Valley. Enthusiasts reopened the line
in 1987 and continue to run it. There are many variations on how you
can use the train – board at Bury and ride the 45 minutes to Rawtenstall, alight there and see the shops, market, Groundwork Countryside Centre, etc. Or you could stop at Summerseat, an attractive
wooded section of the Irwell Valley, or try Ramsbottom, a picturesque
market town, from where you can take an energetic walk to the Peel
Monument or visit the Kipper Cat Museum (see below). The best
thing to do is telephone for or pick up a brochure and work out your
own programme.

Special events throughout the year often include a Mother's Day
Special, Teddy Bears' Picnic, Friends of Thomas the Tank Engine
weekend and Santa Specials.

Huge flights of steps from Bury Station to platforms – the strong
would have to carry pushchairs. Very difficult for disabled people,

but if you telephone in advance there are ways the accommodating railway enthusiasts will get you to the train.

Buffet car on most trains. Refreshments at stations usually available. Toilets on platforms. No nappy changing facilities.

WARNER CINEMAS

Pilsworth, Bury. Programme information. Tel: 0161-766-2440; advanced bookings 0161-766-1121.

M66 junction 3, take road to Bury and exit at signs for Pilsworth Industrial Estate. Free car parking on the flat.

Open Monday to Friday 1.30pm, Saturday and Sunday 11.30am. (Local school holidays open 11.30am). Last film Sunday to Thursday at 10pm. Friday and Saturday late shows start at midnight.

This is a 12-screen multi-plex cinema with all modern facilities and claims to have the largest seating capacity in the country. There are always children's films available, either U or PG, as well as other films to choose from if your children are 12 or 15 and over. A Saturday morning Kids Club starts at 11am and is open to children and adults – 50p for children, adults free. After the film there are games with prizes. You can leave children there if you feel confident enough because staff are always on hand. (There is an Asda Superstore and a Megabowl, see below, opposite).

Be prepared to spend on costly bags of popcorn, Haagen Das ice cream and hot dogs. On the same site is a Mexican Restaurant and a Deep Pan Pizza Restaurant.

Ramps for wheelchairs and space at the back of every auditorium so that a person in a wheelchair can sit next to someone in a seat. There is room for 25 wheelchairs in the largest auditorium.

Toilets, including for the disabled, clear benches in ladies' can be used for nappy changing.

MEGABOWL

Pilsworth Industrial Estate, Bury. Tel: 0161-767-9150

M66 junction 3.

Free car parking on the flat.

Admission prices vary depending on when you visit but expect to pay from £2 to £4 a game.

Open Monday to Friday 10am-midnight; Saturday and Sunday 9am- midnight.

This is a modern, high-tech bowling alley with lots of chrome, neon and glitz. At the entrance is the "arcade" with sophisticated machines to play – many connected with fighting and shooting. Loud pop music, video TV screens above every lane. Unsupervised soft play creche area. Children's parties available with a game, food, host to entertain the party, hats and balloons

Some lanes have fixed bumpers so children can play without the ball ending up in the gulley. Manager recommends age five and upwards. Some youngsters use the metal frame down which the ball can roll, instead of bowling it. These are there really for disabled people to use. There is good disabled access with ramps to the diner, ramps to lanes and all help given. Wheelchairs and pushchairs welcome.

Diner serving fast food, including junior meals (everything with chips) and bar.

Toilets including for disabled people; no nappy changing or breast feeding facilities.

BURY ART GALLERY AND MUSEUM
Moss Street, Bury. Tel: 0161-705-5878

M66, junction 3 to Bury. Museum located in centre of town. Few signposts.

Car parking in town centre. Short walk from central bus and Metrolink stations.

Open Tuesday to Saturday 10am-5pm. Closed Sunday and Monday.

Admission free.

This is a small but imposing building, approached by a flight of steps. The lower level houses the museum which is attractively set out as an old street with shops. The upper floor houses the art gallery with spacious rooms and interesting exhibitions. The ground floor has the information desk and access through to the public library.

An irritating sign greets you at the entrance to say that pushchairs aren't welcome – please leave them at the desk – although I understand on quiet days a blind eye will be turned. But if you could carry your pushchair and child upstairs there seems (to me) to be no reason at all why access shouldn't be granted. Admittedly space is limited downstairs but, when I called, I was the only person there.

Access for wheelchairs is via Silver Street next to the Textile Hall, where a ramp takes you into the library and from there you can reach the museum. Staff are willing to help disabled people to the upper floor in the service lift. Part of the access problem here of course, is the age of the building.

During the summer holidays there is a Summer Fun activity at the museum which is for children aged from five to 15. It is usually bookable and costs about £1 per session. School visits welcome.

One women's toilet on lower ground floor and one men's on first floor. Access involves steps. No nappy changing facilities.

BURY LIBRARY

Manchester Road, Bury. Tel: 0161-705-5872

Town Centre, adjoins the art gallery and museum.

Town centre car parks.

Open 10am from Monday to Saturday; closes Mon, Tues, Thurs, Fri 5.30 p.m,
Wed 7.30pm, Sat 4.30pm.

Admission free.

A small library trying very hard in cramped conditions. Small section set aside for young children and table area for older children to do homework or research. Activities during some school holidays. Check for details.

Access for pushchairs and wheelchairs via a ramp from Silver Street/Manchester Road. Toilets in adjoining museum and art gallery – see above.

BURY TOWN CENTRE SHOPPING

Good shopping centre with wide pedestrian precincts and pleasant indoor centre at Miller Gate – both good for pushchair and wheelchair access. MacDonalds, Pizza Hut and several pleasant cafes. Indoor market has toilets, including one for disabled people, as well as a good nappy changing room. No feeding facilities, however, and access narrow from the market. Baby changing and feeding room in Boots – very welcome, but very cramped. Nappy changing available at Mac-Donalds, but only one person at a time. Mothercare staff say mothers can use cubicles for feeding or nappy changing – but no handwashing facilities.

THE MET ARTS CENTRE

Market Street, Bury. Tel: 0161-761-2261

This theatre, studio, craft centre and cafe bar complex offers a variety of entertainment including music, drama and dance. It also has some excellent productions throughout the year especially for children which are well worth attending.

Contact the above number or Tourist Information on 0161-705-5111.

KIPPER'S CATS OF RAMSBOTTOM

The Pet Shop, Bridge Street, Ramsbottom, Bury BL0 9AD. Tel: 01706-822133

Above The Pet Shop in one of the town's main shopping streets. Arrive on the East Lancashire Railway from Bury (see above) or by car or bus from Bury.

Car parks and off-street parking.

Adults £1, children 50p, families £2.50.

Open Monday to Saturday 9am-5pm; Sunday 10am-4.30pm.

This is an unusual collection of cat memorabilia, set out in what used to be the living accommodation above the pet shop. Kipper is the name of the cat who has lived there since 1980 and has always acted as if he owned the place. So the display was named after him although it was collected by Sylvia Taylor whose family run the shop. There are cat ornaments, jigsaws, books, slippers, newspaper cuttings – everything you could think of – and all attractively displayed with humour. There is an extra large cat flap for children to crawl through and a few buttons to press; also a small table and chairs for children to use, with paper and crayons. Small but fun.

The owner will allow desperate visitors to use his toilet. Pleasant cafe with highchair next door and other cafes in the town.

BURRS COUNTRY PARK

Woodhill Road, Bury. Burrs Activity Centre contact 0161-764-9649. For information contact the Croal/Irwell Valley Warden Service 01204-71561. Bury Tourist Information, 0161-705-5111.

M62 junction 18, M66 to Bury. Leave at junction 2 for Bury town centre. Follow signs for Bolton A58, then signs for Ramsbottom on B6124. Quarter of a mile from Bury town centre turn right on Woodhill Road. The site is at the end of this road. Poor or non-existent signposting.

Open all year.

Admission free.

Parking.

This is an old industrial site which was at its busiest in the early 1800s when water power was used for the mills there. A grand scheme is underway to reclaim the land and make a gateway to the upper Irwell Valley. There are walks in the countryside, a camp site has been provided, and because of the moving water, it is a particularly good site for canoeing. When complete, canoeing facilities will include a regional grade 2 and 3 slalom, a training pool, a figure of eight circuit incorporating the slalom and the southern end of the canoe trail which currently runs for some five miles down the Irwell from Ramsbottom. It is also intended to develop the areas for fishing. The surviving cottages on the site are being renovated to provide facilities for visitors and canoeists.

When you reach the end of Woodhill Road, there is a pleasant, fenced playing field and playground with soft surfaces – dogs not allowed. You can go straight ahead and park and take a walk from there, but if you want to see the new car parking, the renovated cottages etc. take the left fork along a cobbled road.

At the end of this road is the Brown Cow pub, built as a farm in 1752. It opens lunchtimes and evenings and serves meals. Near the end of Woodhill Road is the Garsdale pub which opens lunchtimes and evenings and serves food. There is a beer garden with imaginative children's play equipment on grass.

Other than at the pubs, the site offered no toilet facilities when we visited, but naturally these are planned.

TAMESIDE

PARK BRIDGE VISITOR CENTRE

The Stables, Park Bridge, Ashton-under-Lyne, OL6 8AQ. Tel: 0161-330-9613

A627 Oldham to Ashton Road; turn left if coming from Oldham along Park Bridge Road (signposted.)

Open Tuesday to Friday 1pm-4pm.

Free parking.

Free admission.

Old stables have been turned into an excellent visitor centre showing children all about the natural history of the area. There is a crawly tunnel for brave youngsters to negotiate with a head torch showing what "life" is like under a stone. A timetable with lots of interesting activities throughout the year – leaflets available from Tourist Information (0161-627-1024) or the centre itself. There are canal-side walks north and south and you can walk to Daisy Nook Country Park (see Oldham section) by taking a footpath under the A627. Toilets including for disabled people but no nappy changing facilities.

WERNETH LOW COUNTRY PARK

Lower Higham Visitor Centre, Higham Lane, Hyde, Cheshire SK14 5LR. Tel: 0161-368-6667

From the A560 Mottram Old Road (Stockport to Hattersley/Mottram road). Signposted. Buses from Marple 383,384,388. From Manchester Piccadilly Gardens 210 bus. For further details ring Busline on 01298-23098 or GMPTE on 0161-228-7811.

Open seven days a week throughout the year. Visitor Centre open Tuesday 11.45am-4pm, weekends and Bank Holidays 12.30pm-4.30pm.

Admission free. Free parking.

The park is 200 acres of hill land rising 900 feet above sea level with

84

spectacular views in all directions to include the Cheshire Plain, the Peak District Hills, North Wales mountains and the whole of Greater Manchester. These can be seen by climbing to the War Memorial on one of the pathways through the park. (Take your binoculars!)

It's a lovely place to walk, lots of fresh air and paths are being improved all the time. It's possible to get a pushchair round most of it – although paths can be muddy at times – and there are routes wheelchairs can follow.

The herb garden has been made with raised beds so that wheelchair users can especially enjoy it. The orchard is dog-free so children can play safely. Picnics can be eaten here or at one if the picnic tables en route.

Lower Higham Farm building has been renovated and converted into a delightful visitor centre with flagged floors, seating, displays and etc. Tea, coffee and biscuits are available when open. Toilets, including for disabled people. Wide tiled window ledge in the ladies' could be used for nappy changing.

Helpful warden will show disabled visitors which paths to take. You can also park at two other places and gain access to the footpaths – at Cock Brow or near the quarry, both on the Werneth Low Road from Compsall.

STALYBRIDGE COUNTRY PARK AND OAKGATES VISITOR CENTRE

Hartley Street, off Huddersfield Road, Stalybridge, Tameside SK15 3DR.
Tel: 0161-338-8200

Off the B6175 Huddersfield road, one mile north of Stalybridge. Turning on the right in a dip and bend in the B6175.

Park open all year, visitor centre open Saturday and Sunday 12.30pm-4.30pm.

Admission free.

Car parking

This is a developing country park based on two valleys running up into the Pennine moors. There are walks round the park and out into open moorland, keeping to the footpaths. The country park warden service run guided walks and other events throughout the year. Telephone for details. Small visitor centre with displays. Toilets available when centre is open.

LYMEFIELD INFORMATION CENTRE AND BROAD MILLS

Off Lower Market Street, Broadbottom, Hyde, Cheshire SK14 6AG.
Tel: 01457 765780

In Broadbottom village, one-and-a-half miles south of A57 between Hyde and Glossop.

Information Centre open Saturday and Sunday, please check times. Broad Mills open at all times.

Free admission.

Free parking.

The information centre has countryside exhibitions and leaflets on local interest trails and walks. The Etherow Goyt Valley warden service run various countryside events from there throughout the year. Telephone for details.

Broad Mills is the site of a former large cotton mill – two minutes walk from Lymefield Information Centre. (Parking at centre.) This is an attractive riverside area, laid out with paths and picnic areas. Information panels explaining how the mill operated and the remains of the mills, with their complex arrangement of mill races and sluices, have been restored for visitors to enjoy. Leaflet available from the Etherow Goyt Valley wardens – telephone as above.

TAME VALLEY WAY

This is a varied 21-mile walk which can be broken down into easy stages. It goes from Denshaw, five miles north east of Oldham to Stockport. Guide book available from Tameside Valley Warden Service 0161-342-3306.

PORTLAND BASIN INDUSTRIAL HERITAGE CENTRE

1, Portland Place, Portland Street South, Ashton-under-Lyne, OL6 7SY.
Tel: 0161-308-3374

In the centre of Ashton on Portland Street South.

Open summer 10am-6pm Tuesday to Saturday and Sunday noon-6pm. Winter Tuesday to Saturday 10am-6pm, Sunday noon-4pm. Closed Mondays.

Car parking in the town.

Free admission.

Three main canals built during the industrial revolution join at Portland Basin where there is now a heritage centre. The displays tell the social and industrial history of Tameside with everything from cotton spinning to fish and chips. It has a fully-restored water wheel, a programme of exhibitions and easy access to the Tame Valley and canal walks. School parties welcome by appointment.

Access for disabled people. Toilets, but not for disabled people.

Vending machine for refreshments. Nearby Asda supermarket has small cafe.

Heritage Cruises operate from here for nine months of the year with public trips at weekends. Can be booked privately at other times.

EASTWOOD RSPB RESERVE

Off Mottram Road, Stalybridge. Tel: 01484-861148

Short distance from Stalybridge town centre, the entrance is off the Mottram Road, A6018 between the Hare and Hounds pub and Stalybridge Celtic Football Club.

Admission free.

Car parking.

Open all year.

This is one of the oldest Royal Society for the Protection of Birds' reserves in the country and it adjoins Cheetham Park. Contact the warden for further details.

FURTHER AFIELD

ALTON TOWERS

Alton, Staffordshire, ST10 4DB.

Tel: 01538-703344; Information line 01538-702200

12 miles east of Stoke on Trent off B5032. Signposted from M1 junction 24 northbound and junction 16 southbound.

Open March to November from 9am to one hour after rides close which varies according to the time of year. Special late opening until 8pm during school summer holidays.

Grounds only open during the winter except Christmas Day.

Free car parking, including disabled.

Admission March-May: adults £14,children £10.50. May-November: adults £15, children £11. Children under four free. Second day ticket for £5. Prices are all inclusive of parking, attractions and shows.

This is Britain's only world-rated leisure park with more than 125 rides and attractions which blend into the 500 acres of one of Britain's finest country estates. Although it is well-suited to older children there are areas which are perfect for young ones, so you can take the whole family even if you have wide age ranges. In Fantasy World, Kiddies Kingdom and the Farm there is lots to do and see and for children under 1-2 metres tall there is soft play, a ball pool, bouncy castle, radio mobiles, nets to climb etc. And there's a special section for children under 14. Two new rides are Nemesis, a fearsome, challenging ride for adults and older children and Toyland Tours which is an enchanted dark ride taking guests to a toy factory.

There are lots of places to eat – a la carte, family eating, fast food and speciality kiosks. Highchairs are available at some venues and staff will heat baby bottles. Feeder cups are available at the medical centre.

Plenty of toilets, easy access and disabled toilets, nappy changing, places for breastfeeding.

Wheelchair and pushchair access to all the park – wheelchair pushers allowed in free. There is also wheelchair, pushchair and locker hire.

DELAMERE FOREST AND CYCLE HIRE

Linmere, Delamere, Cheshire. Tel: 01625-572681

Signposted from the A556 Chester road, about 10 miles from Chester. Wayfarer buses 0161 228 7811; BR enquiries 0161 832 8353; Cheshire bus enquiries 01244 602666.

Open 10am-6pm every Saturday and Sunday from April to September, Bank Holidays and every day during July and August.

Cycle hire from £3. Proof of identity required. Returnable deposit. Children under 16 must be accompanied by an adult.

Free parking.

If you're visiting Chester, this is a great place to stop for half a day or more for either a walk or a bike ride – or both. Delamere Forest is owned by the Forestry Commission and has several woodland pathways for leisurely walks. The Forestry Commission Visitor Centre has regular displays about the history of the forest and its current management. The cycle hire shop is next to the visitor centre. A leaflet is given to every hirer so you can choose from the routes available and people are encouraged to bring a picnic so baskets on the front of the bikes are provided.

There are mainly small-wheeled bikes for hire which can be ridden by people with different abilities. Adults bikes can be fitted with baby seats at no extra cost; a bucket seat for 6-18 months and a larger seat for children up to four years. Children's bikes available too. You can of course take your own bike and ride for free.

Forestry Commission Centre serves drinks and snacks and visiting vans provide ice cream etc.

Toilets, no nappy-changing, but disabled facility.

QUARRY BANK MILL

Styal, Cheshire SK9 4LA. Tel: 01625 527468

Junction 5 M56; follow airport signs and then signs to Styal Country Park. Open all year. Twenty minutes from Manchester city centre.

Summer 11am-6pm (last admission 4.30pm). Winter 11am-5pm (last admission 3.30pm). Closed Mondays in winter from October until the end of March.

Complicated admission prices depending on which of the two attractions (or both) you wish to visit. For example, adult (1994) admittance to mill is £3.50, apprentice house £3, combined ticket £4.50. There are concessions for children, groups, schools and there is a family ticket.

Car parking

Access from car park is down steep steps – difficult for both wheel-chairs and pushchairs. But longer way round, down metalled road, safer and easier.

There are two areas to visit – the mill and the apprentice house and both are charged separately or you can buy a combined ticket (see above.) The mill was built in 1784, powered by water to spin and later weave cotton. It is now managed for the National Trust by Quarry Bank Mill Trust Ltd., and is restored to working order. There are three floors of textile machinery and demonstrations of hand spinning. weaving and so on. Impossible for pushchairs. Step lift available for wheelchair users to see the entire social history floor. Access to water-wheel can be arranged. A leaflet for disabled visitors is available from the Visitor Services Manager at the above address.

At the Apprentice House you will find life going on just as it did 160 years ago. Excellent for school visits.

Exhibitions and special events take place throughout the year. Ask for leaflet.

The Mill Kitchen serves wholesome food. Highchairs, will heat up bottle and baby food. Children's menu. Wheelchair access; thick-handled cutlery available.

Mill Shop selling National Trust type goods.

Toilets, including for disabled people which doubles as a nappy-changing room, therefore access for pushchair.

STYAL COUNTRY PARK

Styal, Cheshire, SK9 4LA. Tel: 01625 527468

Follow directions as above for Quarry Bank Mill.

Open all year.

Car parking.

Free admission.

The 275-acre country park is a beautiful place for a family stroll or a longer walk. There are the southern woods and the northern woods to visit. For the southern woods, go from the car park down to the mill and a track leads from the mill yard. There is a fast-flowing river so watch children. You can take a short 15 minute walk round a large pond or go on and return via the river bank – not more than an hour's walk.

The Northern woods offer better walking and are extremely beautiful in autumn. Paths can often be muddy. Pushchair access possible; wheelchairs with some difficulty but access is to be improved.

A leaflet giving details of the footpaths is available at the car park kiosk. The Mill Kitchen (see above) offers refreshments.

Toilets, including disabled and nappy-changing, at the Mill.

TATTON CYCLE HIRE.

Tatton Park, Knutsford, Cheshire.

Tel: 01625-572681

Off the M6 and M56 at Knutsford. Junction 19, M6. Follow signs to Tatton Park. Special buses run on summer Sundays. Wayfarer buses 0161 228 7811; BR enquiries 0161 832 8353; Cheshire Bus enquiries 01244 602666.

Closed Mondays. Open from Easter to October, every Saturday and Sunday, Bank Holidays and every day during July and August. Opens 10.30am mid-April to September; later and earlier opens 11am. Closes 6pm.

Three hour hire from £3. Children under 16 must be accompanied by an adult. Proof of identity required. Returnable deposit.

Cars are charged admission to the park, pedestrians free.

This is specially to encourage families to get on two wheels so there are lots of family bikes – adults' large and small-wheeled bikes and bikes for children from five upwards. Also bucket seats for babies and another type for children up to four years. No extra cost for a child seat. Duet cycle available for one disabled person and one able-bodied person. Helmets available. Baskets for picnics. There are three routes to choose from in Tatton Park and leaflets are given to the hirers so they can choose. You can of course bring your own bike.

National Trust restaurant with disabled access; highchairs.

Toilets at Tatton including for the disabled; no nappy-changing facilities.

TATTON PARK

Knutsford, Cheshire WA16 6QN . Tel: 01565 654822

Three miles north of Knutsford; four miles from Altrincham; five miles from M6, junction 19; three miles from M56, junction 7. Signposted from A556. Station: Knutsford, three mile walk to Mansion and Gardens. Cheshire bus enquiries: 01244 602666.

Opening times vary considerably, so please check first. But as a general guide during April to September, most parts open from 10.30am to 5pm or later; mansion opens at noon. From September to Easter, noon-4pm.

Various prices for different attractions. Explorer ticket can save you money on both first and second visits – please check. Under fives generally free.
Cars £2. Free parking for disabled people.

Tatton Park is a very full day out for there is so much to see and do. There is the Mansion and gardens, the Home Farm, the deer park and meres and the children's playground – not forgetting the restaurant and shop!

The Mansion, though wonderful, is not the best place for small children, but they could enjoy the 50 acres of exotic gardens. Or leave these to granny and granddad and take the children to the Home Farm where little has changed for 60 years. Some animals wander freely and there is always plenty to see and do for children. There is also the Old Hall, a guided tour which transports you through five centuries. Adventure playground with soft surfaces. Walk in the park, see the deer or watch the windsurfing on the mere.

Cycle hire at the Stableyard (see above.)

Rangers dressed in green roam the park; they are qualified first aiders and are glad to help.

Lots of special events throughout the year including a Children's Week in August.

Restaurant expensive but good. Highchairs and will heat up baby food etc.

Tatton park is difficult for wheelchairs but where possible, provision has been made. There are five wheelchairs plus one motorised chair to borrow (book in advance.) Car parking free with disabled sticker. Gravel paths in some areas make pushing a pushchair awkward too. Toilets for disabled people at Knutsford entrance and Stableyard car park. Nappy-changing facilities in ladies' loo; mother-and-baby room also available for breast feeding. Ask at the Information Centre.

CHILDREN'S WORLD

Alban Retail Park, Hawleys Lane, Warrington, Cheshire, WA2 8TP. Tel: 01925-413258

Junction 9, M62. Head towards Warrington, at the second roundabout turn right, then first right into car park.

Open Monday to Friday 10am-8pm, Saturday 9am-6pm, Sunday 10am-5pm. (Sunday opening may change due to new regulations.)

Free car parking.

Free admission.

Children's World stores belong to the Boots group and offer everything for the under-sevens under one roof – toys, games, clothes, baby requisites, prams, pushchairs, play-pens etc. The Warrington store also has a hairdressers, Clark's shoe shop and play areas for children with a slide and play mats. It is an excellent way to shop with young children – they can have a good time too.

Access on the flat from the car park and very easy for pushchairs and wheelchairs throughout the store.

Snack bar has highchairs, feeder cups, will warm baby bottles, has non-fizzy drinks. Food on Sundays is limited.

Toilets, including small toilets for young children as well as low-level wash basins and hand dryers. Mother-and-baby room has cubicles for breast feeding and excellent nappy changing facilities. (Other shops would do well to take note of these facilities.)

EUREKA! THE MUSEUM FOR CHILDREN

Discovery Road, Halifax, HX1 2NE. Tel: 01422-330069 or recorded information line – 01426-983191

M62, exit 24, follow signs for Halifax and then the brown signs for Eureka!. Next door to Halifax railway station. Five minutes walk from Halifax town centre.

Open seven days a week, all year round – closed Christmas Day. Monday 10am-2pm (Mondays 10am-5pm during Eureka! school holidays – check they coincide with yours.)

Tuesday 10am-5pm, Wednesday 10am-7pm, rest of the week 10am-5pm.

Pay and display car parking for 300 cars nearby. But access from the car park on the flat. Disabled parking next to building.

Admission: Children 3-12 £3.50, adults and over 12s £4.50. Under threes free. Small group saver ticket.

Eureka! is Britain's first hands-on museum designed especially for children up to the age of 12. It's won several awards since it was opened by the Prince of Wales in July 1992. Wherever you go you can touch, listen and even smell as well as look. It's a place where parents can relax because you never have to say:"Don't touch!" There are so many things to see and do that this is a whole day experience if you can stand the pace. My children never tire of it. There is a mini television studio, a boat with flares and life-jackets, all kinds of communication devices including a fax machine, a bank, a mini Marks and Spencer complete with mini trolleys and "food", a factory production line and a large "explore the human body" exhibition. There's a small, under-fives play area with a slide and a ball pool. Special activities at certain times of the year.

Trouble is, it's so good, it's too popular and on busy days your visit may be restricted to three hours. Best advice is to get there at 10am because many of the activities are spoiled by too many children being around.

There's a place to hang coats (very useful) and leave pushchairs, or you can take your pushchair round the whole place, using the lift to the upper floor. Wheelchair users are similarly welcome.

A cafe serves drinks and hot food, is child friendly with children's menus, baby food, heaters to warm milk etc. You can eat a picnic in the Eureka! park but not inside the museum.

Toilets on both floors, three disabled toilets, nappy changing and breast feeding facilities.

JODRELL BANK SCIENCE CENTRE AND ARBORETUM

Macclesfield, Cheshire, SK11 9DL. Tel: 01477-571339.

M6 junction 18, A535 Holmes-Chapel-Chelford Road. Look out for the giant telescope and follow Jodrell Bank signs.

Open from third weekend in March to last weekend in October, daily 10.30am-5.30pm. Winter weekends and Christmas holidays except Christmas Day, 11am-4.30pm. Last admission one hour before closing.

Large car park

Admission: adults £3.50, concessions £2.50, children £1.90. Under fives free but not admitted to the Planetarium.

This is a bright, lively and fun experience for all the family, although under fives cannot go into the Planetarium for safety reasons. There is plenty for them to do otherwise however and they greatly enjoy the hands-on activities. But older children will thrill to the size of the Lovell radio telescope, big as the dome of St Paul's and the second largest in the world. You can learn about how the earth's position in space affects your daily life and many more things about earth and space.

Outside there are 35 acres of trees, with pond life, flowers and wildlife to see and there are trails to follow with an illustrated map. There's a picnic area, a children's adventure playground and an environmental discovery centre.

Access throughout with pushchairs and wheelchairs.

Cafe with highchairs and non-fizzy drinks.

Toilets in the main building and the cafe, including disabled toilets, nappy changing and breast feeding facilities.

THE PIECE HALL AND CALDERDALE INDUSTRIAL MUSEUM

Woolshops, Halifax, West Yorkshire, HX1 1RE. Tel: 01422-358087

Follow brown tourist signs from M62, junction 26 or 24. In Halifax town centre, 500 yards from railway station and short walk from bus station. Three main entrances including from Woolshops and from Market Street.

Piece Hall open 10am-5pm seven days a week. Museum open Tuesday to Saturday 10am-5pm. Sunday 2pm-5pm.

Parking in Sainsbury's car park or other town centre car parks. Free disabled parking at Westgate entrance. Pedestrian access only into Piece Hall.

Admission free but admission charge to Industrial Museum within the Piece Hall.

A unique 18th century cloth hall with cobbled courtyards and colonnades. Now filled with small and interesting shops selling everything from art and craft to antiques and bric a brac. Three weekly markets, Thurs, Fri and Sat and special events on Sundays April to September. It's a great place to browse and traffic free for small children. Shops are not too exciting for children – although some sell dolls and toys – but the events can be great fun. Most of these are free and include activities for children too. Check with Tourist Information (01422-368725).

The Industrial Museum makes a small charge for entrance but is more suitable to older children than the under fives. It has many working exhibits and a fun but spooky area representing street life of days gone by. It's on three floors and the stairs are steep and impossible with a pushchair – ask to use the lift. Wheelchair access is best from Square Road where there is a ramp.

Cobbled courtyard in Piece Hall makes it very difficult indeed for pushchairs and wheelchairs. The Hall is on three floors with balconies around and these are smooth but narrow. A lift near the Tourist Information Centre can be used.

Cafe, not operated by the council, offers children's portions, highchairs, babies bottles warmed, non-fizzy drinks. Picnics can be eaten on grassy areas in courtyard.

Toilets, including two for disabled people. Ask at Piece Hall office for nappy changing and feeding facilities.

CHILDREN'S BOOKSHOP AND TEA SHOP

37-39, Lidget Street, Lindley, Huddersfield, HO3 3JF.

Tel: 01484-658013

M62 junction 24, take A629 for quarter of a mile to traffic lights; immediately after turn right at Holly Bank Road, continue until shop comes into view at top.

Open 9am-5pm Monday to Saturday.

Free parking opposite.

Free admission.

Although not a day out, this shop is worth knowing about if you have children. The shop is owner-managed by Sonia Benster and she and her staff read most of the books and know instantly which book would suit a child you describe, if you're looking for a present. It claims to be the largest specialist children's bookshop in the North of England. A hospitable shop for children, it welcomes pushchairs into the shop even though it is cramped. Carpeted floor for babies to crawl, play-pen, bean bags for disabled children to rest, some toys, and books to read while children wait for adults.

Next door is a vegetarian cafe, with highchair, feeder cups, bottle warming facilities and non-fizzy drinks.

Difficult for pushchairs and wheelchairs because it is small but staff would help. One toilet – difficult access. Baby changing and feeding facilities arranged if necessary.

There is a small park opposite, but it might be worth seeking out Greenhead Park, about two miles away at Trinity Street, Huddersfield. (Ask the bookshop for directions.) This is a large pleasant park with an enclosed children's playground, wonderful for the under fives with soft surface and small equipment. In summer there is a small children's fair with merry-go-rounds at modest prices for little ones. Picnic tables, plenty of grass but plenty of dog dirt. Tennis courts, crazy golf. Pushchair and wheelchair access throughout and a good park for safe biking for little ones. Toilets near tennis courts – poor access. Shop open in summer selling drinks, ices etc.

IKEA

Gemini Retail Park, 910, Europa Boulevard, Warrington, WAJ 5TY.
Tel: 01925-655889

M62, junction 9: take A49 towards Warrington, right at first roundabout into Cromwell Avenue, right again at second roundabout near Toys 'R' Us.

Open Mon to Fri 10am-8pm, Sat 9am-6pm, Sun 11am-5pm.

Car parking and disabled.

Free admission

Ikea is a Swedish store selling good furniture and household requisites as well as a small selection of toys. We include it, not so much for what it sells, but for the facilities for the family shopper. Pushchair and wheelchair access throughout the store and pushchairs available for free hire. Free ball pool and games room for the over threes to be left to play for 20 minutes while you shop – nowhere near long enough but it's better than nothing! A Tannoy system calls you back if there is a problem or your time is up. Small play area, unsupervised, within the store for very young children. Free, unsupervised children's video room, first aid post and small but well fitted nappy changing room with feeding chair for one. Excellent toilets for disabled people.

Cafe is tailor-made for families – although if you are on your own with children, the cafeteria system could cause problems. Plenty of highchairs, small tables and chairs, a Lego table, feeder cups, children's portions, a children's picnic bag etc. The cafe has toilets with nappy changing facilities in both the men's and the women's!

Very near Gulliver's World if you want to visit both in a day.

HOLMFIRTH

Holmfirth's own tourist information centre – 01484-687603

From Huddersfield, it's seven miles along A616 Sheffield Road. Buses from Huddersfield (01484 546926) or by rail (01484-531226).

Shops open all week but only cafes and gift shops on Sundays.

Short stay car parking at Towngate, Garpike Estate and Huddersfield road – meters. Long stay at Crown Bottom off Huddersfield Road.

Although a small town and not an attraction as such, many people enjoy a day out in Holmfirth, especially because of its connection with The Last of the Summer Wine television show. But be prepared for narrow pavements, steps and steep slopes if you take a pushchair. Lots of interesting shops, some quite up market, and many of them aren't keen to welcome children with ice creams or grubby fingers. Several events throughout the year including Holmfirth Folk Festival, usually in May.

General market on Thursdays at Crown Bottom and craft market from March to Christmas on Saturdays and Bank Holidays.

Some small cafes in the town including the one used in the television programme and another one called The Wrinkled Stocking, which is on the site of Nora Batty's house. The Old Bridge Hotel does bar snacks.

HOLMFIRTH POSTCARD MUSEUM (01484-682231) is above the library on Huddersfield Road and is fascinating for adults but a little boring for children. Wheelchairs and pushchairs can use the lift because there are two steep flights of stairs. Good toilet facilities and an interesting little shop.

Also in Holmfirth is The Summer Wine exhibition with souvenirs but also props from the programme. However, this is threatened with closure. Presently it's at 60A, Huddersfield Road and is approached down small, stone steps, so access for disabled people is impossible. Check if it's open by telephoning: 01484-681362.

ROCKWATER BIRD CONSERVATION CENTRE

Rockwater, Foxstones Lane, Cliviger, Burnley, Lancashire. Tel: 01282-415016

A646 Todmorden road; turn off for Mereclough at Foxstones Lane; signposted to Rockwater. Bus route from Burnley to Todmorden.

Free car park.

Open Easter to October 11am-7pm. Closed Monday and Thursday except Bank Holidays.

Adults £2, children £1. Party reductions.

This is a rural, low-key, friendly place set up by the owners. Spacious aviaries house all types of birds including pheasants, waterfowl, ornamental poultry, birds of prey, fancy pigeons, foreign birds and children's pets. Corn is 10p a bag. Children can have a good time here, looking at the birds and enjoying the outdoors. There is a small "classroom" where school parties are welcome by appointment. Benches to sit on, lovely views. Rough, uneven pathways make it impossible for wheelchairs and pushchairs, but small enough for toddlers to walk round.

Picnic area. Small cafe selling drinks and biscuits only.

Toilets – not for disabled and no nappy changing facilities.

NATIONAL MUSEUM OF PHOTOGRAPHY, FILM AND TELEVISION

Pictureville, Bradford, BD1 1NQ.
Box Office: 01274-732277; Information 01274-307610.

Well signposted from major routes into the city centre. City centre location with nearby pay-and-display parking facilities, but expect difficulty at busy times. Free parking after 5 pm. Eight parking spaces for disabled people at the museum.

Open Tuesday to Sunday 10.30am-6pm. Closed Mondays. Special exhibitions open until 8pm.

Admission free to museum: from about £3 to IMAX.

The museum makes a splendid family attraction but there are only one or two items which will be of interest to the under fives, although there are plenty of buttons to press and toddlers will enjoy the magic carpet ride. The film theatre, IMAX, with its large screen film experience is well worth a visit but it depends on the attention span of your child. Older children will be enthralled. Some films last 40 minutes and are particularly suitable for youngsters – but the effects can be frightening.

The museum is not ideal for pushchairs because it is on different levels, but you can use the lift or the disabled stair lift. Pushchairs and wheelchairs are welcome however, but there may be difficulty at busy times.

The wine and coffee bar has a children's menu during school holidays, one highchair, will warm bottles, has feeder cups and non-fizzy drinks are available. There is a picnic site.

FUREVER FELINE

(opening December 1994)

Windhill Manor, Leeds Road, Shipley, West Yorkshire BD18 1BP.
Tel: 01274-592955

From Bradford (M606) take A650 then A6038 towards Otley. Turn right at Shipley on the A657. Furever Felime is on the left, 250 yards along this road.

Opening times – to be decided.

Car parking for up to 50 cars including disabled.

Admission: from £2.25, under twos free.

This new exhibition is being set up in the former home of The World and Sooty. (Sooty is moving to a new location yet to be revealed!) It promises to have all the previous facilities of Sooty World plus a new layout, and an additional floor. According to the company behind the scheme, it will be a state of the art animated three dimensional exhibition, featuring cats, which will be appreciated by all ages of animal lovers.

It promises to have ramps and easy access for pushchairs and the disabled, as well as toilets for disabled people and nappy changing facilities. A cafe will serve sandwiches and hot and cold drinks.

WALKLEY'S CLOGS

Canal Wharf Sawmills, Burnley Road, Hebden Bridge, West Yorkshire HX7 8NR
Tel: 01422-842061
About eight miles from Halifax on the main road A646 just before the town of
Hebden Bridge.
Opens all year round, weekdays 9am-5pm, weekends 9am-5.30pm.
Free car parking for 300 cars – but may have to pay at busy times.
Admission free.

Britain's only clog manufacturers, this is a huge mill filled with displays, gifts, furniture, linens, clothing, traditional crafts – beautifully set out in quaint little shops. There is an extremely small ball pool where children can let off steam for 15 minutes or so, but the most exciting place for them is on the top floor – the Enchanted Wood. It has a breathtaking display of European Christmas and Easter decorations with several life-size moving models and figures. Children love it – some smaller ones may be a little apprehensive. Meet the talking reindeer and see a snoozing Santa.

Difficult for pushchairs and impossible for wheelchairs. Lift to all floors. Restaurant serving hot and cold food, high chairs, will heat up baby food. Toilets. Nappy changing facilities and place for breast feeding mothers.

SHIBDEN HALL AND PARK

Godley Lane, Halifax. Tel: 01422-352246.
A58 Leeds Road, know locally as Godley Lane, about one and a half miles from
Halifax. Buses from Halifax bus station.
Free car parks, but lower one from A58 is approached through the park so watch
out for speed ramps and children. This is the best car park for the park itself, but if
you want the house use the car park off Shibden Hall Road.
Modest admission prices.
Hall open March to November, Monday to Friday 10am-5pm, Sunday noon- 5pm;
February Sundays only 2pm-5pm. Closed December and January. Park open all
year.

The hall is a small, homely house first built in 1420. Well worth a visit but not, perhaps, with very young children. It is very difficult with pushchairs. Special folk and craft days are held throughout the year at the hall. Modest cafe selling hot food and snacks. Toilets. No nappy changing facilities.

There are acres of rolling parkland on a very steep, sloped site with a boating lake at the foot of the hill. Footpaths on the flat from the A58 car park are wide and easy for pushchairs and wheelchairs. Earth path round the lake may be difficult at times. Children's playground, children's paddle boats and rowing boats for hire and other attractions during the summer months. Picnic tables, ducks to feed. Delightful train ride through park. Special events throughout the year.

Toilets near lower end of park but no nappy changing facilities. Radar toilet for disabled.

GULLIVER'S WORLD

Gullivers World Ltd., Warrington, Cheshire, WA5 5YZ. Recorded information 01925-444888, or 01925-240085

Signposted from M62, junction 9; M6, junction 21a.

Open every day from April to September; usually just weekends late September and October. Open local October half term. 10.30am-5.30pm. Check before setting out.

Free car park on flat grassy area.. Admission £4.50 adult and child. 1994 season. Children under three feet tall free.

This is tailor-made for families with children from tots to early teens. None of the big scary rides here, but plenty of fun, even for the very young. Set in landscaped grounds surrounding a lake. Boating, log flume, Bodge City Fort, roundabouts, small cars, the "runaway" train etc. Ball pool and soft play area for small children. Shows at various times of the day. The site is flat so ideal for wheelchairs and push-chairs. Disabled children and groups are welcome and although none of the rides are specifically for disabled people, attendants have been trained to help. School parties.

Fast food available. Lots of places to picnic if the weather is fine. Toilets, baby changing room in Count's Castle near the First Aid Station, where a mother can breast feed. Toilets for disabled people at entrance plaza and Count's Castle.

CHESTER ZOO AND GARDENS

Upton-by-Chester, CH2 1LH. Tel: 01244-380280

Zoo signposted along A41 Upton-by-Chester, two miles north of Chester. Bus services from Chester centre. Nearest station is Bache – 20 minute walk from there or take the bus.

Open daily from 10am. Closing times seasonal. Closed Christmas Day.

Check for up-to-date prices but expect to pay from £6.50 for adults, £4 for children, family ticket for five £22. Under threes free.

Free parking well organised on opposite side of small lane which leads to zoo.

Large zoo, stocked full of interesting animals large and small and plenty to interest children of all ages. The chimps are a favourite but so are the large animals likes lions and elephants. Summertime water bus, children's play area, children's farm and children's activities at certain times. A full day out.

Mostly on the flat so excellent for pushchairs and wheelchairs. Wheelchairs, pushchairs and reins for hire. Plenty of toilets with easy access for all. Three mother and baby rooms.

Kiosks, cafeteria, restaurant, tea room, bar, beer garden, facilities for picnics under cover.

KEIGHLEY AND WORTH VALLEY RAILWAY

Passengers can board trains at Keighley, Ingrow West, Oakworth, Haworth, Oxenhope. Well signposted. Talking Timetable, tel: 01535-647777.

Open school holidays and every weekend of the year; weekdays during June to September. Check with Talking Timetable.

Telephone for detailed fares, but approx £5.50 adult day rover. Under fives free.

Car parking varies – free at Oxenhope, paid for at Haworth.

This is a delightful, award winning steam railway and is a super way to enjoy a day out in the area. You can simply take a return journey which will take about one hour or you can choose where to alight and enjoy the facilities there, before catching a later train back again. Santa Specials at Christmas and usually Thomas the Tank Engine arrives in June.

At Oxenhope the station itself is worth a wander – it has a delightful shop geared towards children and refreshments are served in a buffet car at the station. Oakworth is the home of "The Railway Children" film and Damems is the smallest British station. See the carriage museum at Ingrow Station or check out the Bronte history at Haworth.

There are usually snacks available at each terminus or you can find cafes and pubs in the villages or Keighley itself. Picnic areas at some stations. Toilets, but little for disabled people and no nappy changing facilities. However it is pointed out that the railway is run entirely by volunteers and is self-financing so they do their best.

NAGS HEAD – CHARLIE CHALK FUN FACTORY

Chester Road, Little Bollington, near Altrincham, Cheshire, WA14 3RY. Tel: 01565-830486

M56, junction 7 to Little Bollington. (Not to be confused with Bollington near Macclesfield.)

Open Monday to Saturday 11am-11pm, Sunday noon-10pm. Free admission.

This is a family pub owned by Brewers Fayre which has a welcome for children and lots for them to do while parents eat or drink. The accent is on eating, however. There is a children's menu, vegetarian dishes and a range of dishes from the menu for adults as well as blackboard specials. Inside the newly furbished pub is a Charlie Chalk Fun Factory which is a large soft play area for children up to about eight years. The kids can have fun bouncing around while you have a quiet drink or a meal. There is also a large outdoor play area with soft surfaces suitable for toddlers and up to age 14. Plenty of seating for parents out here too. There are toilets for disabled people, nappy changing facilities, highchairs and staff will heat up babies' food or bottles.

BOLLINGTON DISCOVERY CENTRE, CYCLE HIRE AND CANOE HIRE

Groundwork Discovery Centre, Adelphi Mill, Bollington, near Macclesfield, Cheshire. Tel: 01625-572681

Signposted from the A523 Stockport Road. In Bollington turn into Grimshaw Lane at the Waggon and Horses. Buses from Macclesfield and Stockport stop at the pub, then 300 metre walk.

Parking, free admission.

There is lots to do at Bollington. Certainly worth a Great Day Out. We mention the Discovery Centre, Cycle Hire and Canoe Hire, but there are also walks including an interpretive walk so it's worth going there to decide what you want to do. You can book in advance for bikes and canoes which is recommended at busy times.

THE DISCOVERY CENTRE is open 2pm-4.30pm weekdays and 10am-4.30pm weekends and Bank Holidays.

The centre has changing exhibitions, all of which are accessible to children and families and connected with the outdoors, or more grandly, our planet. There is a shop selling tourist and environmental information, guide books and local books, and gifts are usually made from recycled paper, or wood from sustainable forests. There is a children's play table with pens, paper, jigsaws etc. Canned drinks and sweets for sale. Toilets, including for disabled people, but no nappy changing facilities.

CYCLE HIRE opens Easter to October every weekend and Bank Holidays; seven days a week in July and August. From 10am-6pm. Various sizes of mountain bikes are available for hire at prices starting from £3. A deposit and proof of identity is required. No unaccompanied children under 16. The Middlewood Way (see Stockport) is ideal for a traffic-free cycle ride and the most popular route is the four miles from Bollington to Higher Poynton for refreshments. You could take a picnic in a back pack or use the Barge Inn next door to the centre which has a family room and sells food. There are also pubs and cafes in Bollington.

CANOE HIRE may be open every day during July and August but at other times by appointment only. Check before setting out. Booking is recommended especially at weekends. There are four-seater open Canadians from £15 and single seater kayaks from £5 to hire for three hours, part of which time is spend in tuition. Staff on the water give instructions and guidance for half an hour or more depending on ability, and then it's up to you. There are no navigational problems along this stretch of the countryside. Safety equipment and buoyancy aids are available and the age limit is two years to eighty years. Wear loose, comfortable clothing – and take waterproofs.

MANCHESTER AIRPORT AVIATION VIEWING PARK
Ringway, Greater Manchester

Off the A538 Altrincham Road, between the airport tunnel and Wilmslow Moat House.

Open every day except Christmas Day from 8.30am Closing time displayed at entrance.

Parking.

Car park (charge).

The Aviation Viewing Park is on the site of an old brickworks and was transformed by Manchester Airport PLC in 1992. It has spectacular views of the airport and planes which can be seen from your car or you can walk to the higher viewing mound. On average there are 180 take-offs and 180 landings every day. The area includes scrub woodland, wetland and grassland rich in wild flowers. There is wheelchair and pushchair access all round the site, toilets including for disabled people, an aviation shop and a picnic area. There is a Ranger available and an information caravan. Allow 20 minutes for the complete circular walk. School groups are welcome. Ring the Bollin Valley Project 01625-534790 for more details.

MANCHESTER AIRPORT (*see under* Manchester)

INDEX

More Sigma Leisure books for a GREAT DAY OUT!

Also by Janet Smith:
Great Days Out, Derbyshire & The Peak District: £4.95
Great Days Out, West Yorkshire: £4.95

A selection from our current catalogue:

Cycle UK! The essential guide to leisure cycling, Les Lumsdon: £9.95
Cycling in The Lake District, John Wood: £7.95
Off-Beat Cycling in The Peak District, Clive Smith: £6.95
More Off-Beat Cycling in The Peak District, Clive Smith: £6.95
Crypts, Caves and Catacombs, Graham McEwan: £6.95
West Pennine Walks, Mike Cresswell: £7.95
Rambles around Manchester, Mike Cresswell: £5.95
Pub Walks in Lancashire, Neil Coates: £6.95
Pub Walks in The Lake District, Neil Coates: £6.95
Pub Walks on Merseyside, Norman James & Abigail Bristow: £6.95
Best Pub Walks in and around Manchester, Colin Speakman *et al*: £6.95
The Red Rose Walk, Tom Schofield: £6.95
The Two Roses Way, Peter Billington *et al*: £6.95
Traditional Pubs of Old Lancashire, Peter Barnes: £7.95
Liverpool Alehouses: including The Wirral, Michael Anderson: £6.95
Reflections on Lancaster, Terry Potter: £6.95
Reflections on Blackpool, Terry Potter: £6.95
Reflections on Preston, Terry Potter: £6.95
Portrait of Manchester, John Creighton: £6.95
Ghosts, Traditions & Legends of Old Lancashire, Ken Howarth: £7.95
Mysteries of The Mersey Valley, Peter Hough & Jenny Randles: £7.95

You can buy all of these books from your local bookshop or – if more convenient – direct from us by post, phone or fax (add £1 towards postage). Cheques payable to Sigma Press. Access/Visa are welcome
SIGMA PRESS, 1 SOUTH OAK LANE, WILMSLOW, CHESHIRE SK9 6AR
Phone: 0625-531035; Fax: 0625-536800
Free catalogue of over 150 Sigma Leisure books available!